HOW TO
STAND UP AN
M&A
FUNCTION

A complete guide with templates and
perspectives from 50+ practitioners

KISON PATEL   JOHN MORADA

How to Stand Up an M&A Function

Copyright © 2022 by Kison Patel & John Morada.

M&A Science www.mascience.com

How to Stand Up an M&A Function / Kison Patel & John Morada. -- 1st ed.

Hardback: 978-1-7334745-5-9
Paperback: 978-1-7334745-6-6

Table of Contents

Introduction

Talking with customers every day is a delight. We get to learn about their work, their backgrounds, and their aspirations. And of late, encountering corporate development practitioners new to their role has been a trend. During a call and DealRoom demo in early Q2, a young gentleman confided that the first time he would be a transaction lead was the first time he would be on a deal on his own. Although hesitant, he was quite excited about taking on the new role. He was elevated into the role from being head of a business unit. And the corporate investment thesis is planned for 3-4 acquisitions this year. His time spent with us was more valuable than simply looking at software. His time with us was about helping him, considering all the moving parts to building an M&A function from scratch.

While that may seem exciting, building out an M&A function is not easy, especially if you have no previous experience. They sought playbooks or guidelines on how to do it or searched for seasoned peers who could give them 15 minutes of their time. Yet, stringing it all together still makes hearts pause as to whether they are truly starting down the yellow brick road.

This gap in the industry prompted us to write this book.

At M&A Science, our mission is to identify proven techniques and return best practices to our fellow practitioners. Over the past two years, M&A Science has grown from a unidirectional podcast to a worldwide community of contributors.

We want to be able to guide people, of all levels, on how to stand up an M&A function in their organization and execute their deals efficiently to get the best possible outcome.

We are not saying that we are experts who know everything in M&A. However, with the contribution of some of the most passionate M&A professionals, we were able to compile their experiences and knowledge to guide our newest practitioners.

Understanding that not everyone can watch all the episodes of our podcast, we wanted this book to reflect all the knowledge gathered from the platform. Our community of contributors, who generously gave their time and shared their knowledge in the interest of moving the industry forward, must be given credit. This book would not have been possible without their help.

Whether you are prepping for your first deal, or this is your 100th deal, we hope you find this book helpful.

Let's get started.

Chapter 1

Building a Corporate Development Function

This chapter is dedicated to the CEO of the company or the senior executive tasked to stand up the function.

If you are still early in thinking about spinning up a corporate development ("corp dev") function, then allow me to aid in some of that analysis.

First, you don't need to build a corporate development function. You can outsource the entire deal from start to finish, as long as there is a dedicated deal sponsor who is willing to take ownership of the deal.

Second, ask yourself what your new corporate development team will be doing when not working on a deal. Could this team possibly perform other value-add work, such as running a full transaction lifecycle rather than just the front-end buy activities?

Third, a corp dev team may not be in the cards if you want a company to acquire you in the next five years. Back to my earlier point, outsourcing the function may save you the time and effort needed only to turn around and shut it down. The effort to build strong corp dev workflows is not a turnkey project. Expect to invest several months, if not quarters, in this build-out.

On the flip side, having an in-house corporate development function adds significant value to M&A execution. If there are dedicated people who understand your company, then you can effectively select and acquire other businesses. So, if you are looking to build your own function, this chapter is for you.

If you are already hired as the head of corp dev, I suggest skipping to chapter 2.

Section 1.1: Purpose of Corporate Development Function

The corp dev function is more than just doing M&A. The primary role of this function is to better position a company for growth, which comes in different forms.

One form is to assess thoroughly what your company needs to achieve the next stage of growth. They can be in charge of building this capability or often finding and evaluating companies that will help you achieve your strategic goals. They are also responsible for determining whether or not it's in the company's best interest to acquire the entity or just partner up with them.

Another role of this function is to rebalance your company's business portfolio. It is their responsibility to assess non-performing assets and divest these businesses to maximize the company's resources.

Lastly, it is corporate development's role to reduce the exposure of the company to risks and make the organization more sustainable.

Have a clear understanding of the intentions when building out this function because that will ultimately dictate who to hire as the head of corp dev.

The most important thing is the alignment of the corporate development function with the corporate objectives, whatever that may be.

> ## Corp Dev that Fits your Strategy
>
> *"Corp Dev must not only understand the strategy, but they have to believe in it. If they're not on board, then there's going to be problems in the targets that they're looking at."*
>
> **— Charles Breed, VP of Corporate Development at Corel Corporation**

In short, hire based on what you need. Everyone looks at a transaction through their personal lens and expertise. Therefore, filling those roles with the right people is crucial. According to Charles Breed, there are three types of people in the M&A world:

- **Deal Experts** - They usually are previous bankers who are adept at executing multiple deals in a year. They know how to move fast and how to get deals done. They also have a network of peers in the industry.

- **Industry Experts** - These are people who have high operational expertise and experience in a particular sector.

- **Integration Experts** - Managerial experts who have extensive experience in integrating businesses and organizing cross-functional dependencies.

If you are a smaller company, you may have to have one or two people wearing those three hats. However, if you want to be a serial acquirer who does multiple deals in a year, it would be best to have three separate people with that expertise.

You can also hire internal and external people to fill the corp dev team. Hiring internal people will shorten the learning curve since that person already knows the inner workings of the organization. Hence, this is best suited for finding an integration expert. They also have existing relationships with the people inside, so working with them should be a lot easier.

However, external people also have their advantages, and they are the ones who are more updated in the industry. They are not confined inside the four walls of your organization and will bring a new perspective.

Whoever you choose what's important is that they have the right knowledge and skills to fulfill their responsibilities according to your needs.

Just be careful that you don't hire people from direct competitors. That could cause legal problems since competitors will not take it lightly that you hired someone who knows their operations.

Section 1.2: Hiring a Head of Corporate Development

The corp dev function starts with the hiring of the head of the corp dev department. As the name suggests, this person will be responsible for building the business line(s) to whatever avenue he/she/they deem necessary.

The head of corp dev will be in charge of assimilating or developing the inorganic growth strategy of the company since it will dictate the targets that you will be looking at and how to build the M&A team.

If you are looking at massive volumes of transactions, hiring a banker as the head of corp dev would be great. However, if you are looking at a few very transformative deals, it would be best to hire an industry expert and groom their corp dev operational methods.

An industry expert would know how your business works. An industry expert will also be able to source deals effectively since they can identify the right company, technology, and people to pursue.

Deal Experts vs. Industry Experts

"70, 80, 90% of corp dev people have done a tour of duty through Goldman Sachs, JP Morgan, Merrill, Bank of America, or maybe in the venture, private equity side and their transaction people.

There's nothing wrong with that but ask them if they've ever done many large-scale post-merger integrations. None. They usually don't do that kind of stuff, and they don't know technology either.

So, if you are going for volume where you really want to do a lot of transaction deals, bring in someone with that background. But if you can't afford to make a mistake, and those mistakes are made on the front end, hire an industry expert. Someone who can look at the right tech and the right people."

— Charles Breed, VP of Corporate Development at Corel Corporation

Here are some of the key skills required for a Head of Corp Dev:

1. **Good communication skills** – Arguably the most important skill corporate development needs is a strong interpersonal skill set. This role entails extensive reporting with the executive leaders and board members. He/She/They need to have good communication skills to explain deals to higher management while working with the functions across the entire organization.

   Approaching targets can also be delicate. You need someone who can be likable and won't drive away targets because they don't have social skills.

2. **Self-awareness** - The task of the head of corp dev will be to hire and assemble the M&A team. This person needs to be honest about their strengths and weaknesses, in order to hire the right people to fill the skills gaps.

3. **Humility** - Someone is needed who doesn't pretend to know things that they don't know. They must be able to ask for help on things when needed.

4. **Good Leadership** - A strong leader must know how to delegate tasks and rally a team to finish deals.

5. **Objective** - Corp dev cannot champion a deal. They need to remove bias and be objective when assessing deals.

6. **Good understanding of legal vernacular** - The head of the department must understand what a transaction looks like. They need to be able to navigate through the legalities and restrictions of legal documents. Understanding the responsibilities of an NDA, what are binding and non-binding documents, and how to work around those documents is crucial.

7. **Diligent at financial modeling** - Needs to be proficient at handling spreadsheets with a focus on modeling various financial scenarios.

8. **Attentive to stakeholder needs** - Leading corp dev means being part of the greater executive team. Hence, working with other department heads is vital. However, getting along with them by being responsive is a white-glove service.

9. **Having a macroeconomic perspective and a microeconomic point of view** - Many buy plans fall short because microeconomics weighted the market analysis. When Boards ask the tough questions on how an acquisition or divestiture creates value globally, then corp dev falls short. Thorough analysis means knowing the triggers that move macroeconomic markets which have a trickle-down impact on microeconomics.

10. **Knowing the modern M&A lifecycle** - In my conversations with newer M&A teams, I find that their holistic thinking from sourcing to go-to-market spans beyond the strategic but truly weaves itself down into the details. What's even more compelling is how their mentors also think this way.

Section 1.3: Operational Structure

After finding a head of corp dev, formalize the operational structure. Some companies have the head of M&A report to the CFO. This makes sense because you will be spending a large amount of money in a single transaction and will need clearance from your CFO.

However, there can be a conflict of interest since the CFO is evaluating all of the investments of the entire organization. As a result, they might not be able to see the bigger picture in the value of the acquisition. Having your corp dev directly report to you is always a good option, especially for smaller companies. You know the strategy well and won't have any conflict of interest.

For bigger companies where many executives are reporting to you, that approach might not be sustainable. Establish your corp dev within the hierarchy of all the other executives, so that the function will have a voice in the organization.

Otherwise, they're always going to think of corp dev as a subservient group. Therefore, they won't have the necessary trust and credibility to provide strategic initiatives around growth.

Establishing Trust and Credibility for Corp Dev

"Corporate Development has to be associated and tied to the executive level decision making of the organization. That doesn't necessarily mean that the corporate development representative is a C-level person, but they need to have a seat at that table.

I have that direct experience before where I had a seat at the table with the eight other functional area executives and the CEO.

We determined where we were going to place our bets as a company.

Where we wanted to grow.

How we used M&A to complement that strategy.

Having that seat at the table led the M&A practice and the strategy and corporate development to really align well with the overall growth trajectory and the objectives of the business so that our deals were successful.

You had buy-in from all functional areas, from the executive leadership group on down, so that when issues came up, you had support from all the functional areas and all the leaders of the company to fix problems and integrate the business."

— Scott Kaeser, Head of Corporate Development at First Choice Dental Lab

Section 1.4: Supporting a New Team

CEOs should also be engaged in the review and analysis of companies. It is not the corporate development's job to sponsor acquisitions. You can't just leave all the responsibility to the new M&A team. Avoid putting them in a poor position where they can be used as a scapegoat and blamed for every bad acquisition.

Avoid being the only deal sponsor or champion for acquisitions. It's not scalable, considering that you have a day job aside from doing M&A. Involve other people from different functions, depending on the type of acquisitions completed.

The business leaders that will be inheriting or running the acquired business post-close are typically the best deal sponsors. They know the business well and will be responsible for it after the deal is done. Therefore, having them champion the deal makes more sense.

Chapter 2

Developing Corporate Development Muscle

This chapter will resonate the most with those in a newly hired head of corp dev role.

As the head of the corp dev, it is your responsibility to strengthen the function and build a team to effectively grow the company, so it can reach its full potential. Here are a couple of ways to do that:

Section 2.1: Understanding the Company

Your first job as the head of corporate development is to do due diligence from within. There is an old proverb that essentially equates to, "Before one can lead the future, one must first master the past." By holistically understanding your new business, the context of operations and the content of tribal knowledge are at your fingertips.

Steps to Developing Strategy

"Number one, understand the business. Number two, meet the people. And then number three, understand the process that they're currently going through.

I can't stress enough how important it is to really understand the core business.

- *What products are you selling?*

- *What services are you selling?*

- *What's the value proposition?*

- *What makes your company better than its competitors?*

- *How do the back office and the supply chain work?*

- *How does the sales team sell?*

- *What is their go-to market?*

When a sales guy is out there, I want to meet these salespeople. I want to meet our department leaders; I want to meet everybody in the business and just talk to them about the business. Understand how it works, the model, how we make money, what our competitive advantages are, all sorts of stuff.

I spent 30 days probably interviewing department heads, meeting people, flying to this location, driving to that location and meeting folks and introducing myself, and really just learning about the business.

If you talk about trying to go and buy a business, how are you going to buy a business, plug it into your business, if you don't even really have an understanding of what you're doing."

**— Michael Palumbo, Director of Corporate Development,
HALO Branded Solutions**

Gathering context entails numerous meetings with people across the entire organization, from top to bottom. M&A touches every facet of the organization, so it will have an impact on various functions, whether or not they are directly involved in the transaction.

Meeting with every function will help you fully understand your entire company before you can start putting your formal M&A process down on paper. Have a good handle on aspects like:

- company culture

- grasping the value system and cultural assumptions

- who are the senior leaders that are going to play major roles in deals?

- what are the existing policies, processes, and constraints that are already inside your organization?

- who are the direct influencers and who are the indirect influencers, and (just as important), who are the blockers?

- understanding motivations and triggers

- why things get done a certain way?

- who are the important customers benefiting from an acquisition or divestiture?

- which vendors would be impacted by a transaction?

- which federal, state, and local agencies regulate your business?

These considerations should shape and affect how you do transactions.

During the journey to understanding the business, work with others in the organization to set expectations of the role and the plans to create growth value for the company. It's very common for people to not know what corp dev is and why you are asking all these questions. Building relationships with the people you work with is imperative because these are the people that will help you get deals done.

Here's an overview of the first 60 days:

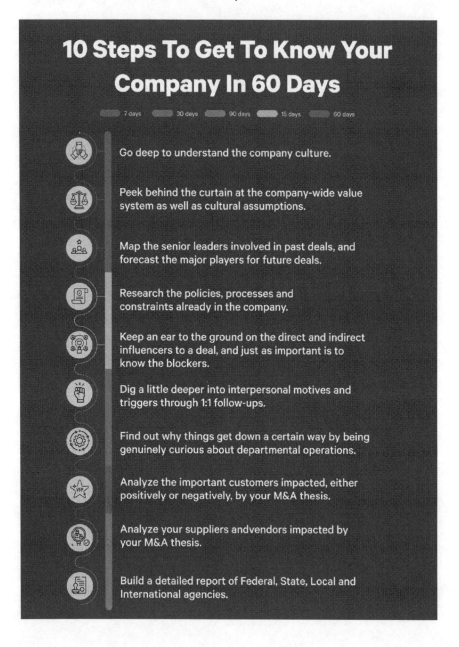

Section 2.2: Building your Network

One of the major roles of being the head of corp dev is relationship building. Whether it is internal or external relationships, cultivating and nurturing relationships is the key to your success. This is why you need to have good interpersonal skills, to begin with. If no one likes you, no one will do a deal with you.

Internal Relationships

Relationships start within a company. Have several meetings with the senior executives about the corporate strategy and what you are trying to accomplish in the role.

Remember to work with the business leaders. After all, they are going to be the deal sponsors. You and the business leaders must be on the same page as to what kind of targets you should be looking at and what the corporate strategy should be. The kind of relationship you have with the business sponsor can make or break a deal.

The Importance of Good Relationships with Business Leaders

"In my mind, this is one of the biggest challenges of a corporate development role. It's not sourcing deals, it's not negotiation. You're either setting yourself up for success or failure based on the relationship you have with the business sponsor. Because it drives what strategy you pursue.

How are you going to value these businesses? How are you going to execute it? What are the terms that are important and how are you going to integrate them? Getting that right is that the single biggest thing you can do to make M&A successful"

— Michael Frankel, President and CFO at Trajectory Alpha Acquisition Corp

---

It is easier to have an experienced business leader as the deal champion. If you have a not-so-experienced leader, then educate them about M&A and what it is you are trying to do. Either way, a good relationship is key. A good business leader can keep you in check and could prevent you from making bad decisions.

Another important relationship to have is with the CFO of your own company. Understand their mindset, perspective, and goals, so that you know what kind of deals you can afford. There needs to be a foundational element of respect, understanding, and sharing of the same perspectives.

You need to know if the CFO is aggressive or conservative. When you're working on financial modeling and valuations, make sure that you have taken into account the business leaders and their views on what you'll eventually be presenting as an investment thesis to move forward.

External Relationships

Cultivating external relationships is just as important as internal relationships. Good relationships with people outside your organization can help you source deals, close deals, have easier negotiations, and execute deals. Having a good network of people can result in referrals to companies that refuse to sell their company to you.

Having a vast network of friends might take some work, but it is extremely beneficial. You need to nurture relationships with bankers, private equity people, and consultants. They will have networks that can help in the long run. The last thing you want to happen is to miss out on a great opportunity because you never heard about it.

When building your network, educate the people around you regarding your role - including what you do and what you are looking for.

This can spark ideas or even opportunities that you might not have gotten all on your own.

As you build trust with people and reputation, deals will soon come to you naturally.

Section 2.3: M&A Strategy

When spending time with product managers, senior executives, and business leaders, you get a good sense of the gaps that you can fill to grow the company inorganically.

- Are you going to expand your geographic footprint?
- Are you adding more products?
- Do you plan on consolidating existing fragmented businesses?
- What do your customers need?

Understanding the acquisition strategy will give you a better picture of who your potential targets are and what future acquisitions would look like.

Your strategy can also define how big the corporate development team should be. If you plan on acquiring companies once a quarter, then you need a sizable, dedicated team. If you plan on doing M&A deals occasionally, then a lean M&A team could suffice.

Business leaders frequently just want to start acquiring their competitors to remove competition. While nothing is wrong with that, it may not be the best use of your time and resources. Acquiring competitors does not always allow you to maximize growth and will certainly not transform your organization.

If you want to do transformative M&A, apply future-back thinking. Communicate with the business leaders and have them walk you through what they want their business to look like in the future. You will now be able to work your way backward on the types of deals that you need to be doing to achieve that big picture.

When it comes to formulating an M&A strategy, the main goal is to understand the market and the customer's problem. That's the only way you will be able to generate great value out of a transaction. **Here are Matt Arsenault's (VP of Corporate Development at Jamf,) steps to formulating a strategy.**

1. **Simplify your goal** - What is it that you want to do? What kinds of bridges are you trying to build?

2. **Understand the target market** - How competitive is the market? Is there an overlap of your customers in that market? How far away is that from your core? Perform a SWOT analysis, if necessary.

3. **Plan to get there organically** - Use your customer's voice to navigate how to step into a new space and determine your ability to solve different problems.

4. **Sequencing Opportunities** - With all the potential target markets, you need to narrow it down and identify where to focus. Which one will deliver success?

Remember that buying a company is not a strategy. The strategy needs to determine the targets and not the other way around.

HOW TO STAND UP AN M&A FUNCTION

Future-back Thinking

"Once you find a deal sponsor that has the right objectives in place and the right appetite for getting deals done, then you can start asking,

- *How do you see your business five, seven, or ten years from now?*

- *What is your market position?*

- *What does the offering look like?*

- *What do your capabilities look like?*

- *What problems are you solving for your customers?*

- *What is your geographic footprint?*

- *What does your asset base look like?*

Get them to paint a picture of what the finished product looks like and then work your way backward. Identify what your current business looks like and then the gaps will be fairly obvious. This will help you get a good strategic view of the business and really detail how you are going to get there.

The problem is that business leaders usually have a target in mind, and as they learn more about the target, they let the target dictate the strategy and come up with a story around why the deal makes sense. It is important to get them to develop the vision, the strategy, and the business case for doing M&A first, without any targets in mind."

— *Dustin Intihar, Director, M&A and Strategic Partnerships at Enprotech Corp*

Of course, you also have to assess if you can achieve your strategic goals by building the capabilities yourself. This is why collaborating and working closely with senior management is crucial. You don't want to be wasting your time pursuing a deal that doesn't make sense and will never get the approval of your board.

However, one of the most challenging situations that you might encounter is having to work with business sponsors who lack M&A knowledge. They think M&A is a strategy that will instantly make the company bigger. More crucial, they don't know the importance of integration. They don't have a clear strategy on what to do with the business after you have acquired it.

M&A is Not a Strategy

"M&A by itself is not a strategy. Many times, in the absence of a strategy, companies will try to buy their way into one. That's just a common mistake that you see with operating executives. I think I've seen that throughout my career. I really view M&A as a tool. It's a really powerful tool that can help achieve a company's strategic objectives and really accelerate, achieving those company objectives."

— Sean Corcoran, Senior VP, Corporate Development & M&A at DigiCert, Inc.

This is where you come in. It is your responsibility to educate the business leaders on how M&A works and that there needs to be a clear strategy for each acquisition.

Getting Business Leaders Up to Speed

"Experienced GMs who understand M&A are an amazing pleasure to work with because you get down into the really interesting questions of how are we going to win with this strategy? What are the important characteristics of an acquisition target? Things like that.

With ones that don't, the investment upfront to get them up to speed is worth it because it makes such a big difference. I think of M&A a lot like a waterslide; once you start a process, it's out of your control. You're going at a certain speed, and you can't get off. And getting a business leader prepped for that in advance is much better than trying to do it in flight."

— *Michael Frankel, Michael Frankel, President and CFO at Trajectory Alpha Acquisition Corp*

We all know that business leaders have day jobs and are extremely busy. Unless the deal was their idea, they are not going to have a vested interest in the transaction. However, even if it was their transaction, do they clearly understand the effect of this deal on the organization? Michael Frankel uses a play that solves all these problems.

Play # 1 - Business Sponsor Lab

❖ **Description:** This play is designed to achieve alignment between corp dev and the business leaders.

❖ **Play By:** Michael Frankel, SVP, Managing Director at Deloitte

About the play

There's a lot of dialogue that goes on around an M&A strategy. There are usually a lot of documents back and forth between people who have day jobs. This is a highly inefficient process that usually takes months to get finalized and often produces a disjointed 'mish-mash' result with disparate feedback/ideas from different leaders.

Business leaders who spend five minutes a day thinking about the M&A strategy will often not take it seriously. Most business leaders also think that M&A is an easy process and that they can even do it themselves if they have the time.

Use this play to get instant alignment with the business leaders. Ask them things that they don't know the answer to. Scare them about what could happen and the ramifications of a failed deal.

Get all the business leaders and key people inside a room, lock the door, and take away their laptops or cellphones. This will get them to focus and collaborate. You need to come out of that room with a clear action plan for what everyone needs to know about your own organization, the market, and the target company.

Preparation

People: CEO/Deal sponsor, Corporate Development, Diligence Team, Banker, Consultants

Difficulty: Medium

Materials: Team collaboration, Honesty, Patience, Visual Aids

Time: As long as it takes

Running the play:

1. **Identify the key people.** When your organization is about to do a deal or there is a particular target that the business leaders are starting to get interested in, identify the key individuals that would be involved in the potential deal.

   This usually involves:

   - CEO / Deal Sponsor
   - Project Manager
   - Head of Corp Dev

2. **Preparation day.** After identifying the key people in the potential deal, arrange a meeting with all of them when everyone will be available. Pick a venue that is accessible to everyone. It is preferably an empty room with no distractions and a door with a lock. Visual aids should also be prepared, if necessary. Business leaders will sometimes remember better if they can attach a visual aid to the topic.

3. **Business Quarantine.** You now have all the key people inside the room. Take away their laptops and cellphones to ensure focus. Start asking the hard questions. The goal is to get everyone on the same page about what the M&A strategy of the organization is. What are the plans for the upcoming deal, how should it be integrated, who's going to be the diligence team, who will be the integration leader, etc.

4. **Examination.** Prepare a simple exam to ensure that everyone is on the same page. It could be Q&A, or a written exam.

5. **Follow-Up.** The work done at this session must not be allowed to be forgotten or dropped. Quickly document the findings and views and set out clear, actionable next steps (market research, developing a financial model, building a target pipeline, further socialization in the organization, etc.). Send that back out to participants and get their active agreement and support. You should also identify WHO (outside the CD team) needs to be engaged in the next steps and get their leaders to assign/commit them.

Cisco even includes the integration lead in these initial strategy meetings. They want to make sure that integration understands what the business is trying to accomplish by purchasing a company and what is the end state that they are trying to achieve.

Integration During Strategy Meetings

"The integration and corp dev partnership is absolutely critical. As part of the integration, how do we become part of, not only corp dev strategy but the business strategy?

When our business leaders are reviewing their portfolio and looking at areas that they may need to buy, in order to accelerate progress in a certain portfolio area, we want to have a seat at the table as those discussions are happening. It should be even before the target is selected.

It's not about the integration, that's only secondary. It's about the business and really understanding why we are looking at a certain target. And then looking at the integration as, how are we going to make it happen?

We're not negotiating the deal. However, we are very much part of the deal modeling, having the input as to what success looks like and holding the business leaders accountable, to have clarity on why we are buying the company and what we want to do with it.

From there, we want to build out the integration plan and have complete alignment with the business leaders and with the corp dev team."

— Karen Ashley, Vice President, Corporate Development Integration at Cisco.

Solidifying the M&A Strategy

Just because you and your business leaders come up with an M&A strategy doesn't mean it will work. At this point, it's all conjecture. It is your job as head of corp dev to validate the formulated strategy and determine whether it is solid enough to enable an acquisition.

How do you actually do this? Tomer Stavitsky, Corporate Development, M&A Lead at Intuitive Surgical, does four things:

1. **Learn and anticipate the trend of the target market** The goal is to understand where the current market is, where it is going, what it is about, and to determine the active players.

2. **Talk to the market** After gaining information, talk to the companies in the space to learn more about the market. You could also speak to the users in the space and conduct market studies.

3. **Focus on your thesis** You will now have a clearer picture if your strategy will solve a problem by executing the acquisition.

4. **Monetize the Value** Finally, you must know how your organization will profit from this transaction. It could be additional revenues, lower costs, or even a better experience for users.

Doing this exercise will help validate the strategy and subsequent acquisitions. However, do this exercise frequently, since the market shifts all the time. To keep your strategy fresh and current, try quarterly updates. Even small incremental changes will be helpful.

You can also do a market map exercise. Creating a market map allows you to narrowly focus the M&A priorities and have deeper alignment with the business unit on the overall M&A strategy. It requires collaboration with the business unit leaders, product team, corporate strategy team, and many others. (See illustration below)

DEAL SOURCING - ECOSYSTEM MAP CASE STUDY

Core Software ①

Back Office ②				

Lead Gen / Digital Marketing ①	CRM ✔ ②	CORE ERP Main Vertical 1 ✔ ①	Document Management & Comm ①	Punchlist Management ②
Rebate Programs ③	Surveys ④		Land Development ③	Line Management ④
Design Rendering ⑤	Website Design ⑥	CORE ERP Main Vertical 2 ②	Dashboards ⑤	Reporting ⑥
Site Planning ✔ ⑦	Standalone Sales Office ⑧		E-Signature ⑦	Payroll ⑧
Estimating ①	BIM ②	Bidding ③	Project Management ④	Lead Generation ⑤

Back Office ④

Operations ③

According to Sabeeh Khan, Director of Corporate Development at Infoblox, the objective of market mapping is to increase relevance within the served industry through strategic acquisitions within each industry ecosystem.

How to Create a Market Map

Creating a market map starts by identifying the core solution or product. Then, work with the business unit leaders, product team, strategy team, and many others because they understand the business more than anyone else.

As illustrated above, start surrounding your core offer with the necessary functions to operate it. With the help of the business leaders, break down all the categories into subcategories you need to sell the product, retain customers, and operate the business. Prioritize them and put numbers from highest to lowest, based on total addressable market, technological needs, or market demands.

Lastly, identify and put a checkmark on the ones that you already have. You will now see potential areas to pursue acquisition and list down potential target companies based on the capabilities you need.

Benefits of Market Mapping

- Increase wallet share

- Drive stickiness through deeper penetration into customers' environment

- Add incremental recurring revenue streams through new cross-scll opportunitics

- Accelerate ROI for market share expansion opportunities

- A more purposeful approach to M&A activities

Section 2.4: Deal Origination

Now that you have an acquisition strategy and a good grasp of what your company needs, it's time to build the pipeline. Deals can come from anywhere, even though corp dev owns the list. It can come from business units, investment bankers, investors, private equity sponsors, family, friends, and even existing partnerships that can turn into acquisitions. Your list can get very long and confusing.

Building your Pipeline

"Build a good list of targets first. Don't start so broad that you're trying to boil the ocean; not every company in the world is a target. You also shouldn't get so narrow that you only have a few names on your list. It's going to be a pretty short process to contact those companies.

Find the information to populate your database, from industry associ- ation lists or other lists that are available. They may be free through internet searches, or you sometimes have to pay for the lists.

Improve the information in your database, so each record makes sense from a corporate development standpoint. That means finding out who the owners of each company are and any other useful info you can gather (such as the size of the company, location, and contact info).

Your corporate development efforts will be off to a great start if you have a great database of targets."

— Scott Kaeser, Head of Corporate Development at First Choice Dental Lab

---

This is why you need to create a system for filtering your list. Learn how to screen potential targets effectively, so that you are bringing quality and well-vetted companies to your deal sponsors. The last thing you want to do is burn people out by asking them to review numerous companies that won't make good acquisitions.

Taking out bias and emotions is the number one requirement for filtering a list. Having a profound affinity for a target can cloud your judgment and force you to do a bad deal. One of the best ways to filter your list is through deal size. Some companies will be too small for your business to make an impact, which will be useless to pursue. On the other hand, you shouldn't even bother to look at companies that are too big for you to acquire.

Adding criteria is another good way to filter your list. Group companies based on strategic qualifications, in order to identify the best opportunities for each criterion.

Setting up Criteria for your list

"What you should really focus on, is setting up a set of strategic filtering criteria that's established early in the process, so that you can cut out all the emotion, noise, and the underlying process. It's best to do this before you even set up a separate set of criteria that are more financially oriented.

These filters should also be tailored to the specific company and the business unit. They can include things like increasing distribution or share, targeting large markets, growing markets, accelerating the product roadmap, and adding additional technical capability. There are also even defensive considerations, which are taken into account in these criteria.

Setting up these criteria is really helpful in cutting the noise out of the process because the list can get very long.

Within any company or business unit, there's ideally some sort of regular strategic planning cycle. Whether there are annual or quarterly check-ins and refreshes, it's important that market scanning and candidate identification are topics of that underlying process.

Therefore, you begin to establish a list that ranks and prioritizes different opportunities. It is obviously going to vary from company to company. However, it's also an important part of the process that corporate development gets involved really early in strategy development."

— Sean Corcoran, Senior VP, Corporate Development & M&A at DigiCert, Inc.

Matt Arsenault, VP of Corporate Development at Jamf, uses a scorecard. It serves as a filter and should set out how you look at companies, based on an inward assessment of your ability to enter a market organically, dictated by customers.

Importance of Scorecard

"Every company should have a scorecard for internal, and all corp dev teams should start from that scorecard."

— Matt Arsenault, VP of Corporate Development at Jamf

A scorecard needs to include the metrics that management consistently tracks. If your organization cares a lot about sales metrics, that is what you should base your scorecard on.

However, it doesn't stop there. Consider how hard it is to integrate the target company. This can be measured by identifying the differences between you and the target, which includes culture and other change management aspects.

Aside from the sourcing strategy, one very effective and reliable source of deals is the salespeople that are on the front lines of the business. They know which companies they keep losing to because of specific functionality or technology that your organization doesn't have. You can offer a deal finder's fee for those employees who can find you deals so that everyone is proactively looking for opportunities.

Keep an eye out for businesses that are not for sale. According to Rishabh Mishra, Vice President and Head of Corporate Development at Infostretch, those are the best acquisitions for any buyer. They are focused on growing their business, and there is not as much competetion, which prevents prices from being driven too high.

Sourcing Companies that are Not for Sale

"Traditionally, everybody has believed that M&A is only done in a marketplace where you have a willing buyer and a willing seller. My philosophy is that all entrepreneurs are building businesses that will eventually be sold.

Businesses are legal entities, they are not human, they can perpetually exist, and the shareholders keep changing. Even in a private scenario, you can't expect the founder entrepreneur to run it beyond his lifetime. So eventually, companies get sold.

If you see the companies which are available in the market, most often they have been just up for sale. They are under-invested for growth. The ones that are not for sale are the ones with the maximum potential of growth and are built for the future."

— Rishabh Mishra, Vice President and Head of Corporate Development at Infostretch

---

Section 2.5: Building a Dedicated Corp Dev Team

Now that you have your strategy in place and a list of potential targets, it's time to build your team according to the acquisitions that you are going to make. Surround yourself with the right people for your strategy.

However, while creating a dedicated M&A team has its advantages, it is absolutely crucial to note that you can successfully execute transactions without a dedicated team. There are many external services that can help you finish a deal. Pull in people from the organization, whenever needed. Just be careful, since constantly pulling people from their day jobs can cause burnout, which will affect the performance of the entire company.

However, when building a dedicated corp dev team, work closely with the CFO. The CFO's role is to identify the cost-effectiveness of the corp dev team. It will dictate the budget for hiring dedicated people. The company's size is a major criterion that will indicate how big your dedicated function is. See the chart below and learn what dedicated functions that are appropriate to your company size:

Legends:

✔ - Yes. You need to hire a dedicated M&A person.

M - Matrixed. You borrow people from your company's internal functions.

O - Outsourced

	Startup in Series D or later, looking to grow inorganically	Small company	Mid-cap company growing through inorganic	Large corporation with a single business line and looking to grow inorganically in the next two to three years	Very large company having multiple business segments
M&A Analyst	O	✔	✔	✔	✔
Project Manager	M	✔	✔	✔	✔
HR	M	M	M	M	✔
IT	M	M	M	✔	✔
Supply Chain	M	M	M	✔	✔
Sales	M	M	M	M	M
Customer Support	M	M	M	M	✔
Marketing	M	M	M	M	M
Legal Team	M	M	M	✔	✔
Integration Lead	M	M	M	✔	✔

Depending on the size of your company, you need very few M&A dedicated people. Keep in mind that M&A deals are not a constant thing. There will be dull moments when the pipeline is almost empty. There should never be a large number of people just sitting around waiting for the next deal.

Even if you are an enterprise-level company, start off with matrixed M&A people. First, show and prove that you have an active pipeline before seeking approval to hire dedicated M&A people.

Importance of Dedicated M&A People

"The truth is, corporate teams are generally understaffed, and the investment is just insufficient, especially considering the type of impact that they're looking to achieve.

The areas where you see the greatest complexity, if you're doing professional services, are generally going to be around IT and HR.

Adding resources that are specific to those functional areas that speak M&A, or corporate development can be very helpful. Whether they're hard-lined into the corp dev team or dotted line, doesn't really matter so much as they are dedicated to M&A.

This is also the other key element for capturing corporate lessons learned, so you can leverage them for your next deals."

— **Ken Bond, Head of Corporate Development at Cetera Financial Group**

However, if you have somehow convinced your CEO to approve hiring people, or you've made enough acquisitions to get the budget that you need, then making the right first hire is extremely important.

Hire someone who will stay with the organization for a long time. This is because having retained knowledge from one deal to another is one of the main benefits of having a dedicated team. If you keep replacing people, it defeats the purpose of what you are doing.

Based on the illustration above, here are some of the most common hires to make.

M&A Analyst

Arguably the most important role to fill in the beginning is that of an analyst. Consider this hire within the first 90 days of being the Head of Corp Dev. One of the best potential candidates would be a vice president of an investment bank.

This person is a valuation expert who will help build models of the target companies. They also help in conducting research on prospective firms and preparing presentations to be used in negotiations.

Having this person around also alleviates the rounds of emails with business-line executives to do the exact same thing. Your business peers do not have time to read through assumptions and valuation models. They simply want the shortlist of targets, with an attached buy plan. Let the analyst do the heavy lifting, and your peers will thank you for it.

When hiring an analyst, make sure that he/she/they are adept at the specific industry. M&A valuations rely more heavily on the market approach, which estimates business value based on data from similar companies and transactions.

A dedicated analyst will help retain data gathered on potential target companies and the valuation criteria of your company for every target that you consider. Not having to start from scratch every time you look at a company will improve the speed and efficiency of the entire M&A process.

Project Manager

A project manager is another crucial role. Consider having this person 30 days prior to the close of an acquisition. This person can come from the business, should be well-versed in the business, and have an influential network.

There are also project management professionals who have experience managing integrations that you can outsource and hire for this role. However, if you want to continuously improve your M&A process, hiring a dedicated M&A project manager is highly beneficial.

The project manager's role is to make sure that deal leads are executing the process according to how it's designed. Keeping the team on track is their number one priority all throughout the process.

The project manager needs to have heavy operations experience and a complete understanding of the business. If they are in-house, you don't have to teach your process and governance to everyone each time you acquire a company.

Hiring Process

As simple as it may sound, you'd be surprised how frequently the hiring process goes wrong. This section details the actual steps of hiring a corporate development lead, as discussed by an M&A Science Academy instructor, **Justin Goldman, CFO at Place Exchange.**

Step 1. Write the Job Description

Writing a formal job description with qualifications is crucial to set the right expectations for candidates and to ensure that you find the right person for the job. For instance, the corporate strategy might be to expand internationally, so you'll need someone who is adept at making international deals and has experience dealing with international culture.

Though the strategy might change in the future, it helps if you hire the right person for any immediate needs.

Step 2. Set your Budget

Hiring a Head of Corporate Development can be expensive. However, it is very much worth it. Considering the exponential growth expected from the function, proper compensation should be a priority.

Work with the CFO regarding the budget to identify the range of professionals you can afford. Be upfront about your budget so you don't waste anyone's time.

Step 3. Evaluating the Candidates

While skills are important, cultural fit is equally as important. Corporate development touches a lot of areas in an organization. Therefore, hire someone who works well with others. Have multiple people evaluate the candidates, especially the people who will often work closely with the role.

If there is an existing corporate development team, they should be included in the evaluation. This is important because it will most likely be a relatively small team.

Building Your Corp Dev Team

"It's important for me to find people that I know are going to be able to work well within our company because such a critical part of our role is working cross-functionally. Working with people in finance and engineering, they have different personalities and can have very different approaches.

You need to find people who are comfortable working across all these different functions and where each of the different functions will also be excited and will want to work with me and my team.

Because if they don't want to work with me and my team, my job becomes a lot harder. So, it's super important to me to find people that have a really strong interpersonal skill set, not only working cross-functionally at their level but also up the executive level.

We have a lot of interaction with our board because M&A is such a critical part of our strategy. We have regular dialogue with them on a weekly basis at our executive team meetings."

— *Jeremy Segal, Senior Vice President of Corporate Development at Progress*

Most importantly, you want the right people asking the right questions. Plan who will be asking what questions because the last thing you want is HR asking questions about financial modeling.

Step 4. Build your Pipeline of Candidates

Now that everything is set, it's time to find candidates. The first place to look is your own network for referrals. Not only are referrals easier and faster, but research also shows that the retention rate is higher when someone is hired through a referral. If you can't get any referrals, post the job opening online.

You can also hire from your internal people who want to get into M&A. The good thing about hiring internal people is that they already understand the industry. They will be more efficient at due diligence since they know what to look for and how the target company functions.

They also know the people inside your organization, so in the event that they have to access information from different functions, they will know who to approach. The existing relationship that they already have will also help to ensure cultural fit.

However, the downside in hiring internally is that they probably have no experience in M&A. Therefore, you will have to take time to get them up to speed.

Hiring external people also has its own benefits. External people will have more up-to-date knowledge and expertise regarding the industry and market. Furthermore, they will bring a fresh and different perspective compared to internal people.

Step 5. Prepare your Questions

It is important when you interview to unlock specific soft skills required for the role. It's not enough that he/she/they are capable of handling the job description. Test for communication skills, positive attitude, attention to detail, etc.

What **Justin Goldman, CFO at Place Exchange,** likes to do is spend 30 minutes with the candidate and have them tell their story: What is their background, and why they made certain choices around education and career stops along the way.

Step 6. Give a Case Study

Giving a case study to candidates can be beneficial. First, it can give a sense of the candidate's work ethic. Once hired, are they willing to do extra work? A corp dev role can be taxing and might require long hours of work.

A case study also allows you to see if they can build a model, which is an essential part of the job description. This includes both written and verbal presentation skills. You also can identify if the candidate knows the industry well.

How to Build a Case Study?

1. **Set parameters** - Whether it's real or hypothetical, give the candidates a brief background regarding the strategy, industry, and three potential companies that you are looking to acquire.

2. **Have them evaluate the businesses** - The companies that you provide should be public companies, so they can adequately research information. Make them pick one company and explain why they think it would be a great acquisition. This should include building a financial model, valuation ranges, and diligence items.

3. **Give a 10-day deadline** - It is important to include a weekend in the deadline to find out if they are willing to work extra-long hours since a corp dev role sometimes requires weekends.

Step 7. Check References

Check references before making any hires. Most people check references after they hire the person. That is obviously too late. Prepare a handful of questions ahead of time to avoid forget anything when checking references.

Here are some suggested questions:

- How do you know this person?

- How do their critical thinking skills match up?

- Can this person eventually learn to think outside the box when ready for promotion?

- Tell me about the quality of their work.

- What was their reputation in the company?

- What are their strengths?

- What are their areas for development?

- What motivates them?

- Are they passionate about learning?

- Would you hire them again?

- Is there anything else I should know before I hire this person?

Step 8. Onboarding

After hiring, it's time to set new employees up for success. You can't expect them to perform at the highest level on day one without any preparation. Provide reading materials to get them up to speed, such as newsletters, primers, or research reports regarding the industry.

Introduce the new hire to a list of key people. This is a great opportunity for them to meet new people in the organization, form new relationships, and learn more about the company.

Section 2.6: Setting Up Processes for Inorganic Growth

Having a good team with templates is not enough to create successful acquisitions. A majority of deal failure is because companies are not properly set up for inorganic growth. If you want to be a proactive buyer, organize the company in a way that is easy, simple, and fast to acquire a new entity. Here are the areas that you need to work on according to **Christian Von Bogdandy, Head of M&A at Slalom.**

Playbooks

Repeatable playbooks are a great way to continuously improve the entire process and not start from scratch at the beginning of every deal. The goal is to have a guide for every time you acquire a business. This is very important, especially for smaller companies who do infrequent deals.

If you are only acquiring one or two deals a year, people can forget the process they are supposed to follow. Having something that they can come back to will increase the efficiency and speed of the transactions.

Furthermore, even if you are a larger company, documenting your M&A process is still in your best interest. The last thing you want is to rely on the retained knowledge of employees, who can leave and take the process with them.

When we talk about playbooks, we don't mean a bunch of checklists to hand out to people as a list of things that everybody should start doing. Playbooks are more of a knowledge repository that lists down everything that should be done in a particular workstream. These are the types of things that are the same for every deal that you can pass on to different people or teams.

As an example, we provided a sample workbook below that can be filled up based on a specific industry and acquisition. Ultimately this is what is going to constitute your playbooks.

<u>Strategic Value</u>

Objectives Of the Deal
1. <Enter OKR #1 here>
2. <Enter OKR #2 here>
3. <Enter OKR #3 here>

This should be tied to the deal rationale that was presented to the board.

Value Creation Analysis
1. <Enter OKR #1 here>
2. <Enter OKR #2 here>
3. <Enter OKR #3 here>

What will generate value when done with the acquisition?

<u>Operational Governance</u>

Policies
1.
2.
3.
4.
5.

List all the corporate policies relevant to this workstream effort.

Risk Management	Remediation	Contributor	Probability
1.			
2.			
3.			
4.			
5.			

Document the issues, risks, dependencies, and remediation that are highly impactful to the success of this workstream effort.

Job Architecture

No matter how good playbooks, IMO, or tools are, transactions will result in delays and employees leaving, if you don't have the right people strategy. It's no secret that job titles are extremely important to people. If there are 200 job titles in your organization, acquiring a whole new set of people and giving them positions that they will be happy about will not be easy.

This also directly affects the compensation and benefits package for certain titles. If there are 200 different types of compensation packages, mapping everything out will be messy. As a result, it will greatly slow down the transaction and frustrate employees. Imagine telling newly acquired employees that they have to wait a month before learning what their title is.

In order to be a proactive acquirer, there has to be a simple process to follow. Consolidate the existing roles/position and make clear distinctions between them. Simplify the job architecture to uncomplicate absorbing and acquiring new people.

Decision Making

In order to make integrations work and be successful, integrate as fast as possible. This means making decisions quickly regarding what to do with the target company post-close.

When preparing a company for acquisitions, you need to standardize the governance and decision-making processes to increase speed. In the course of an integration process, there are too many decisions to be made, so a process that is inclusive and fast is required.

- What are you going to do with discrepancies in the compensation of your old employees and newly acquired employees?

- What are you going to do with the facilities of a certain type of transaction?

- What are you going to do with the product names of your newly acquired business?

- What are you going to do with the newly acquired brand?

- What are you going to do with company costs?

These are several examples of decisions that must happen at lightning speed. Either template the actions or create a process on how to decide. The best thing that you can do is document how you are making decisions and build off of that.

Onboarding Process

If you're bringing people into the organization, make the onboarding process efficient and easy. This means having a simple operating model. If the operating model is hard to understand, then the person coming in will have a high learning curve. Imagine 200 people going to work without understanding what they are doing.

To test the simplicity of the operating model, start by asking internal people. Do they understand the structure of the organization and how are things connected? Or do only the leaders understand it?

These are some of the things necessary to set up a company for continuous and efficient acquisitions moving forward.

Data and Systems

The same is true for data and systems. Create a model where data can easily be brought in. For example, if you're buying a company that has the same customer base as your company, which one of those two customer accounts do you keep? How do you merge the data? Figuring these things out is not something you should do in the middle of a deal.

Chris suggests using an Internet platform as a service solution (PaaS) to bring in data faster. This can save two to three months of the integration process.

Corporate Governance

It is imperative to set a gold standard for each acquisition. The perfect example is to never consider a deal that is below an X amount of return, EBITDA, or any other metrics that matter to you. Having this guardrail in your governance is essential to avoiding deal fever.

Limits on Authority

"You want to have limits of authority that are absolutely in place, so you don't get to a situation where a CEO can make a unilateral decision on whether this particular acquisition is the best opportunity for the company.

It starts as far back as analyzing the deal, the potential for growth and finance, and what your rate of return is, based on the modeling that you've done.

So, there's an agreed understanding inside the company that we don't deal with a rate of return that's less than X percentage, for example.

And that rate of return would be derived based on what kind of standard rate of return might be for your industry. You're going to look at all kinds of metrics.

And then based on the size of the deal, you would have an executive team of people, including the CEO and the CFO who review deals and can decide whether the deal meets your metrics.

If it falls within your metrics, then you can move forward. Then once the deal rises to a level of dollar value, for example, a potential purchase price, that is over X, then it has to be approved by the CEO, the CFO, the general council. That's how you set up your limits of authority to make sure that more than one set of eyes is reviewing the deal and making the decision."

— Nichelle Maynard-Elliott,
Independent Board Director at Xerox

Deal Fever

From time to time, sponsors, or even CEOs, experience deal fever. It is an irrational feeling that they must acquire a particular business, ignoring all the potential risks associated with the company.

More commonly, after spending countless hours and resources looking at a deal, it gets harder and harder to walk away. We've all been there. The more time invested in a deal, the more it consumes everyone, and the more you try to convince yourself that this is the right deal for you.

However, your team should not forget the deal rationale. Remind yourself of the very reason why you looked at the company in the first place. Does this transaction advance the corporate strategy?

One of the red flags to watch out for is sponsors that are too optimistic. If the sponsor's projections are too aggressive and are ignoring potential risks without adequate planning, it's vital to have a conversation with them.

Here's a play to use before sending out an LOI.

Play # 2 — Red Team Exercise

❖ **Description** - In this play, Red Team Exercise, learn how to properly assess the deal thesis and combat cognitive decision biases.

❖ **Author** - Jerry Will

About the play

Deal fever is one of the leading causes of failures post-close. Deal sponsors can be biased, especially when the deal originated from them. Without the proper motivation behind a deal, it can cause a lot of wasted time, money, and effort.

The diligence team is often not given the right platform to explain why a potential deal is not in the best interests of the company. This leads to the continuation of the deal without the support and conviction of the deal team.

Preparation

Use this play to properly assess the deal thesis. Assign people to the red team with the sole purpose of tearing down the deal thesis and convincing the deal sponsor not to do the deal. This play will give the naysayers a platform to honestly say what they think about the deal, without facing judgments and backlash.

The red team needs to be able to say or go wherever they want. For this play to be effective, they need to have unrestricted access to data and can use whatever arguments they want to use. This will give you the highest visibility of the deal's potential upsides and downsides. It can also generate additional diligence and pricing theories.

People: CEO/Deal sponsor, Corporate Development, Diligence Team, Banker, Consultants

Materials: Team collaboration, Honesty, Creativity

Difficulty: Medium

Time: 1 hour

Running the Play

1. Assemble the teams

    Upon announcing the deal thesis, assemble the red team and the green team. It is important to find people who don't believe in the deal and put them on the red team. If you can't find any, you can hire an outside consultant to give you an unbiased perspective regarding the deal.

    The green team, on the other hand, is there to protect the deal thesis. Both teams will ideally be composed of three to four people.

- Corp Dev person
- Banker
- Consultant (inside or outside)

2. Preparation

   After the teams assembled time to prepare for their respective arguments.

   For 48 hours before the discussion day, all their cases need to be out in the open for the other team to read. This will give them enough time to prepare for arguments the other team might have for a more productive discussion.

3. Stipulation

   You cannot dispute every fact. There needs to be a stipulation on a common set of facts that both teams can agree on.

   Each team will only have 20 minutes to present their cases. Therefore, it is important to focus on the conversation about the difference in perspective.

4. Discussion Day

   After much research and preparation, it is time to face the jury. Set aside one hour for this play.

   Start with the red team and give them 20 minutes to present their case as to why the deal shouldn't go through. The green team then has 20 minutes to convince the CEO otherwise, and the last 20 minutes are set aside for final discussion.

   At the end of the day, you are all part of one team, and you need to agree on what's best for the company.

Aside from the infamous deal fever, pulling out in the middle of a deal, especially if you went far down the road, can be construed as a failure. This kind of culture forces the deal team to push a bad deal forward, even if they know they have to walk away. They don't want to be the team that wasted all of the company's time and resources.

You can create a culture where you celebrate walking away from a deal. This will encourage your team and organization to be more diligent in every transaction. This is how Duncan Painter does it in their company. He is the CEO of Ascential.

Celebrating a Failed Deal

"Pulling out of a deal is really hard to do, and people don't like doing it because they feel like they've made themselves look silly."

So the one thing that we always do as a company is, if we pull out of a deal really late in the process, which is, of course, where all these tough decisions have to be made, we actually celebrate that deal more than if we do one.

We've encouraged that culture in our teams. We go out and have a bigger celebration if we pull out than if we conclude.

I know it sounds a bit odd, but it's to create a culture in the company where everyone on the team recognizes that being transparent and raising reservations, and raising concerns are encouraged.

And not having to worry that that's somehow going to get frowned upon or be negative about. We want to encourage the exact opposite.

The second they get worried about pulling out, it becomes a problem. I'd rather encourage my teams to celebrate walking away than to celebrate buying a business that becomes a problem down the road."

— Duncan Painter, CEO of Ascential

Gun Jumping Rule

To avoid any legal problems, have a clear guideline on how to coordinate and work with the target company without violating any rules.

Gun jumping is a law that prohibits a buyer and the seller from acting as one entity before the deal is officially closed. In short, this rule doesn't prevent them from planning, but it prevents them from executing plans.

Neither company can attempt to exercise control over the other before closing. Both companies should still operate independently from one another, and all work associated with the integration teams should be deemed confidential.

Below are some examples of activities prohibited under the gun-jumping rule:

1. No joint pricing or promotions.

2. No coordination on competitive decisions or strategies.

3. No influencing each other's day-to-day operations.

4. No joint decision-making.

5. Employees cannot act on behalf of the other company's employees.

6. No coordination of sales, purchasing, or contracts with vendors.

7. No implementation of integration plans prior to closing.

8. No access to office space or sales, marketing, or operational personnel.

Below are some examples of activities allowed before closing:

1. Joint planning of the combined company's post-merger organizational structure.

2. Discuss compensation plans and employee benefits to each other.

3. Discuss financials, tax, IT, environmental, health, or safety issues.

4. Discuss valuation of assets.

5. Discuss regulatory compliance.

6. Interviewing employees

The idea behind the gun-jumping rule is to keep the competitive spirit throughout the entire process. If the deal falls through, both companies will also be able to walk away easier.

Integration Budgeting

Before closing a deal, there should always be an integration budget report. Many companies do not include integration costs as part of their process. They ignore it and assume that the costs go away due to the functional departments that are going to work on the deal.

It's not only unfair to the respective departments, but it is highly inefficient since integration costs can and will affect the overall viability of the deal. The last thing you want to do is expect a certain amount of synergy that has no chance of being realized because the cost of realizing them was too high.

The best thing to do is have the integration lead plan the integration budget early. These costs are an essential input to the valuation model. As the target company sends over more information throughout the process, you can continuously add more information to the valuation model. As a result, this live document becomes more and more accurate. It can help teams properly assess if the target company is worth buying.

Chapter 3

M&A Operating Framework

We dedicate this chapter to the entire M&A team involved in the transaction. In this section of the book, we are going to uncover the entire M&A framework starting from deal sourcing to integration. Best practices are also included on how a team member should approach each of the phases of the deal that they are involved in.

Section 3.1 — Setting up your Framework

HEAD OF CORP DEV

Once you have a solid understanding of the environment in which your M&A function is going to operate, start to define the processes for each major stage of the transaction lifecycle.

Develop standardized processes and templates for each stage of the transaction life cycle. Remember that everyone must understand the rationale behind the framework to get buy-in.

When Building Your Operating Framework

"When building out your processes, you need to be consulting, collaborating with colleagues that represent the major stakeholder functions at your company. They're going to help you avoid potential pitfalls, misunderstandings, and areas of internal controversy that might come out of your processes.

> *Involving all these people is critically important to ultimately get the buy-in across the organization. At the end of the day, you can have the best-laid plans. However, if people don't buy into them, they don't buy into your processes and aren't going to follow them, they don't understand why they exist. You're not going to get anywhere."*
>
> **— Russ Hartz, VP, Corporate Development at Ansys.**

The Traditional Approach

The biggest challenge in M&A is the process itself. People involved in M&A deals are frequently excited at the beginning of the transaction. However, somewhere along the way, due to a lack of efficient processes, their enthusiasm wanes. It usually ends up with frustration, confusion, and a lot of pointing fingers at who is to blame. This is why it's crucial to make the M&A process as efficient as possible.

The traditional waterfall approach is highly inefficient since it is mostly focused on strategies, valuations, and finding the right deal for companies. This approach has caused over half of the successful deals to fail to meet their projected value. They are frequently unable to capture intended synergies, resulting in future spin-offs and divestitures.

Why?

It is because the traditional approach is extremely siloed. The people who created the investment thesis, valuation model, and intended synergies are not part of the integration team.

Why M&A Transactions Fail to Achieve Value

"The biggest problem is the lack of continuity between the corporate development team and the integration team.

Any time there's an acquisition that doesn't meet a certain threshold of size, it seems like it doesn't get the necessary attention that would be required for any other large transactions.

After the transaction gets signed, it seems like the senior leadership loses interest in running that integration program.

The transaction gets thrown over the fence to some management team, or whoever is able to catch it. That group is either ill-prepared, has to do this on top of their day job, or lack the tools, processes, and resources that they should be using in order to achieve successful integration."

— Galina Wolinetz, Managing Director at Virtas Partners
M&A Integration | Separations

Aside from the lack of focus on integration, the traditional approach is also process-oriented and too focused on checklists. While checklists are a good place to start, you can't over-rely on checklists. Crossing out checklist items can be addictive and can give people a false sense of accomplishment.

The Problem with Checklists

"When you have more of a process and checklists, then people start to follow the checklist and work down the list. This is a fantastic feeling that you're getting things accomplished. However, it means that you're not stepping back and thinking about the bigger picture.

Pilots have rigorous checklists, but there's also a stage when a pilot walks around the aircraft and does a general assessment outside of the checklist to make sure that they're ready to fly.

If everybody is thinking about the checklist, then no one is thinking about what is not on the checklist."

— James Harris, Principal, Corporate Development Integration at Google

Being overly dependent on checklists is one of the biggest reasons why functions work in silos. The common mistake is to hand out checklists to team members and just expect them to start crossing out items. However, the reality is almost every workstream or function has interdependencies with another function.

A simple example of this is HR. When HR looks at employee compensation, the legal team has to check the employee contract, and the finance team also needs to verify the numbers. Collaboration is crucial if you want a successful M&A transaction.

Checklists are not bad, but how you use those checklists makes all the difference in the world.

How to use Checklists

"Checklists can be a guide. Think of them as frameworks.

I always tell people, think of them like the bumpers in a bowling lane so the ball doesn't go down into the gutter.

Think of checklists as something to keep you from going into the gutter. However, what are some of those additional things that we need to consider as we go through this process? Where do we really need to keep the pulse?"

— Naomi O'Brien, Head of M&A Integration at Honeywell

Agile M&A

Through experience, companies and practitioners have started focusing on integration. As a result, they have begun to realize that integration creates value.

Importance of Integration

"Big emphasis on Integration is definitely an interesting trend. You'll even see that my role even exists now as an integration-focused person.

We always have corporate development focused on valuation. How much is the deal we're going to get with this company? How it can further our strategy, customer, new customers, new market, new region, but then we're not realizing that there's a huge gap in the "what now?"

> *You have two entirely separate bodies of companies with different operating models, different financials, different approaches to products, and different cultures. There's a huge gap in how you even merge those. it's not an overnight practice, just as I'm sure you've seen in a lot of your conversations. This is like a one-year, three-year, five-year work, and you have corporate development who's onto the next big thing. Leadership, and board of directors want to buy the next big thing to further our strategy even more, but then you have this huge investment that isn't actually seen through.*
>
> *There's so much more Interest and focus now on actually making sure that we get the right ROI for these big investments."*
>
> **— Johanna Tseng, Corporate Development, M&A Integration at Coinbase**

Because of the shortcomings of the traditional approach, world-class M&A practitioners have started using a more goal-oriented, integration-focused approach called Agile M&A. It is a principle that encourages rapid response to change, collaboration, and continual improvement.

In this framework, diligence and integration are one continuous flow. The goal is to reduce the information chasm that happens between stages. We want to be able to encourage integration planning as early as possible so that as new information comes in, the plan continuously gets updated.

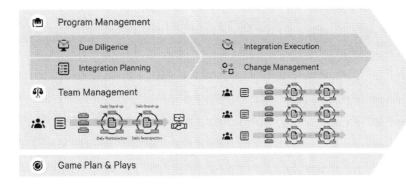

The Agile M&A framework also encourages the use of plays. These are strategies or exercises used to overcome obstacles and achieve specific goals. In its simplest form, it's a structured conversation of how you are going to deliver value or solve the underlying problem. You will see more plays later in this book and learn how to use them to overcome challenges.

Leadership

However, it all starts with leadership. If the leader or leadership team doesn't have the right mindset and attitude to adapt to new ways of working, then none of the team members will. If there is not an environment and a framework that allows employees to be collaborative and adaptive, then the process will suffer.

Importance of Leadership

"The most important factor of all is leadership. If you don't have the leadership, you have nothing. A failure in M&A is a failure in leadership. Period. If you don't have leadership, then nothing else follows. To be successful in this day and age, leaders must embody and act out Agile and innovative ways of working. This is what our leaders must do."

— **Toby Tester, Senior Consultant and Project Manager at BTD**

Leadership often gets overlooked. However, make no mistake, the impact of leadership runs deep. It is the leader's job to keep everyone engaged in the process while keeping their focus on the things that matter in the deal.

The Lack of Focus on Leadership

"There is a ton of effort and riding both on the academic and the consulting side that is kind of exclusively focused on the role of culture in M&A deals. While it's a necessity that organizations need to focus

on and help understand, I think leadership has been subsumed into the culture conversation. In any kind of cultural assessment, we'll have some conversations or questions around what kind of risk management profile do they have? How do they communicate and collaborate? All of these things are leadership related. However, because the culture piece is so large in deals, there's not a lot of attention paid to the focus of leadership and how important it is in a deal.

In fact, we believe that leadership is the foundational element that's going to determine whether your deal succeeds or is falling on the pile of failed deals that are out there in history."

— Dr. J. Keith Dunbar, CEO/Founder of JKD Talent Solutions and FedLearn

---

Establishing Your Framework

Establish your M&A Operating Model based on, but not limited to, the following items on each stage of the deal

Deal Sourcing

- Target Screening
- Approaching the Target Company
- Working with Bankers
- Tech Stack

Documenting your deal

- NDA
- Preliminary Diligence
  - o Diligence List
  - o Valuation Model
- Letter of Intent

Negotiating the Deal

Confirmatory Due Diligence

- Selecting your Integration Lead
- Prioritizing Deliverables
- Due Diligence Team

Integration Planning

- Setting Success Metrics
- Focus on Employee Retention
- Prioritize Go-To-Market Strategy
- Finalize Integration Budgeting
- Perform Premortems

Providing Governance

Day One Preparations

- Communication Plan

Closing

Post-mortem Reviews

- Frequency and Schedule of Post-mortems
- Documentation of Best Practices

Section 3.2: Deal Sourcing

Target Screening

HEAD OF CORP DEV Having everything laid out, it's time to shop. However, picking a target company without integration in mind can be a mistake. The target company might be great and could serve the strategy very well but cannot be integrated properly or effectively into your organization due to various reasons.

There are companies that have started involving their integration lead during the targeting phase to get their input on whether or not to integrate the target company into the organization.

Even though there is an issue regarding confidentiality, involving the integration lead would be extremely beneficial. Integration leads are often the business leaders who will inherit the business post-close unless you have a dedicated Integration Management Office.

However, whether or not you decide to involve the integration lead, it is important to envision how that company is going to fit inside of your organization as soon as you're thinking about acquiring a company. As you progress through the deal, continue to iterate that initial hypothesis and turn it into a thesis.

Integration During Targeting Phase

"Integration should start at the targeting stage; because they should understand and include some of the integration criteria and components into the targeting criteria and profiling of a particular client that you want to target or acquire.

As you bring those integration criteria into the mix, it allows for a better valuation further down the line. It allows you to prevent any risks, and not fall into some of the pitfalls.

> *You don't want to end up in a situation where you've closed the deal and as you're going through the integration, you're opening up the bonnet and you're finding a lot of things."*
>
> **— Javid Moosaji,**
> **M&A Sales Integration Strategy at Paypal**

Another part of an effective target screening process is using third-party data sets. Access to tools such as PitchBook and S&P Capital IQ is a great way to filter targets. These tools give great insight into companies that can be a strong indicator of what you are or are not looking for (size, revenue, scalability, etc.).

Diligence During the Targeting Phase

"We have access to different tools such as PitchBook and Capital IQ so we're able to obtain some data.

For instance, let's say we are interested in a company. When we check them out in PitchBook, we find out that they have ten employees and they've raised $2 million. That target is not very realistic for us because they probably have very little revenue and they're too sub-scale for us to look at. We look for:

- *What kind of fundraising they've done?*

- *How many employees do they have?*

- *Is it a company that would have the level of scale that makes it worthwhile for us to do outreach?*

We can pretty quickly determine whether or not it's going to be a company that's going to fit within the parameters or not.

This exercise is one of the preliminary things that we do because we don't have access to the other factors that are important to us.

— Jeremy Segal, Executive Vice President Corporate
Development at Progress

You also need to involve your legal team, usually in-house counsel. There are many regulatory issues and concerns to know before approaching a certain company. However, in-house counsel can only give sound advice if they know your M&A strategy. Therefore, make sure that they know and understand the deal rationale.

Legal team during targeting phase

"Bring your legal team in as soon as possible. We have a very strong business development team here at LyondellBasell, and thankfully they bring in legal from the beginning.

My team and I are involved in looking at different targets, thinking if those targets are the right fit. My primary role as an attorney for the company is to understand the regulatory, legal, and jurisdictional issues and obstacles that may present themselves with any transaction.

- *Are we going to have issues going to a certain new country and to a certain industry?*

- *Are we going to have antitrust concerns?*

- *Does it involve national security issues?*

You want those issues highlighted and flagged sooner rather than later, because the worst thing that could happen for the company is to spend a lot of time and money looking at a transaction, and then at the very last moment, bring in your legal team, and then they tell you to slow down because you have to do X, Y, Z first."

— Andrew Gratz, Associate General Counsel at LyondellBasell

Approaching the Target Company

HEAD OF CORP DEV

Most people are too eager to call the target and go in unprepared. First impressions are important, and the last thing you want is to ramble and irritate the business owner. During the first call, have a prepared speech ready. It has to be short, succinct, and very clear about your intentions. You might want to start by introducing yourself and asking them out for lunch.

Do not tell them that you want to buy their company, because the reality is, you don't know enough about the company for that to be true. It's a get-to-know-each-other phase, so practice active listening and educate the target about who you are and what your organization does. This phase is crucial because it will determine if they want to meet with you in person or not.

Before setting up the first meeting, you should have already collected enough information about the target to know if it's even worth your time. The last thing you want to do is waste both sides' time and approach someone that is not worth pursuing.

During the first meeting, try to be as productive as possible. Prepare a list of the most important questions that you need to know and cover them in the first meeting. People like to talk about their business, and the only thing that you need to do is listen and gather information.

Importance of Listening

"Once you're meeting with someone, whether it's in their office or over a meal, or just out of the office, they're going to start telling you a lot about their company. What they're looking for, what's good, a lot of times you'll be surprised, they'll start telling you what's bad. As a buyer, I want to know sooner than later

---

> *Listening is vitally important. So covering the five or so topics, having those broader topics or questions that you come armed with, allows the seller to just start talking and elaborating the business about their businesses is key.*
>
> *It makes those meetings go fast. You're talking for an hour. If it's going so well that it takes more than that, great. But you're just letting them talk about their business and listening so that you can structure your deal properly to protect yourself from issues you hear that you may not like, and really learn more about the target."*
>
> — **Scott Kaeser, Owner / Head of Corporate Development at First Choice Dental Lab**

Working with Bankers

HEAD OF CORP DEV

Working with bankers is a great way to source deals. It is especially important if a function is new and doesn't have an active pipeline. Bankers can also inform you of deals that are not on your radar, and the transaction will be more organized, since they know how to handle sell-side transactions.

However, it also has its drawbacks. Bankers typically run an auction process, and a competitive process will not only drive-up prices.t It will also increase risk because speed is a crucial part of winning an auction.

To avoid working with bankers, it is important to foster relationships with companies everywhere and be proactive in your deal sourcing. An important part of your role is to have a good standing relationship with companies that are in the same industry or in an adjacent space, whether they are a potential target or not.

Deals can come from everywhere. You will be maximizing your chance of sourcing acquisitions if you are aware of these deals. Not to mention the fact that people are more likely to sell their business to acquirers that they know and trust.

> ## Importance of Relationships with Target Company
>
> *"It's one of those art, not science things about M&A that I love, and I think it's massively important.*
>
> *I think that relationships with potential targets drive everything, from better diligence to better integration, to easier negotiations, to a higher likelihood of getting the deal done.*
>
> *I spent a lot of time thinking about how to develop those relationships and what makes it both complicated and fun is your strategy and approach totally vary based on the nature of the target and based on the nature of the relationship you want to have with them."*
>
> ### — Michael Frankel, SVP, Managing Director at Deloitte

Good relationships can be beneficial and crucial in a corporate development role. Solid, trustworthy relationships help close deals and enable easier negotiations. Start with the strategy and then identify potential targets or adjacent companies. It is recommended to create relationships with 10 to 15 companies. Focus on a selected group. It's physically impossible to foster meaningful relationships with every player in the market.

Furthermore, it's also important to note that it's not just relationships with decision-makers that are important. There are other critical parties in the organization to consider, such as unique talent that can be crucial in an acquisition.

> ## Relationships as a Separating Factor
>
> *"The way that we do math around deals is very standardized. And even after all the work, LOIs will fundamentally look the same, the management incentive packages look functionally the same, and in a hot market, the winner will win by an eighth of an inch in terms of pricing.*
>
> *There is so much commonality in terms of valuation and the way that the deals are structured is not how you're going to differentiate yourself.*
>
> *At the end of the day, you have to lead with trust. And values, character, and friendship matter."*
>
> ## — Jay Jester, Partner at Plexus Capital, LLC

Finally, this will also give the potential target a view of a company's values and culture. This is important because most sellers want to know that their employees are taken care of after the acquisition. A good relationship will destroy the gap and distrust between the buyer and the seller.

Tech Stack

Technology has evolved rapidly over the years. There are now many available tools out there that can, and will, help the M&A process be a lot smoother. As a matter of fact, you no longer even need to be in the same room in order to work together.

However, changes and new technologies aren't always quickly embraced by people. You need a good amount of leadership in order to implement these tools. At the end of the day, you need buy-in from all of your members for it to work.

Importance of People embracing Tools

"Whatever tools you have, if you don't have willing participants and people that are open to that type of working model, it's not gonna work."

— Christina Amiry, Chief of Staff to the COO at Atlassian.

Atlassian is one of the very first companies to go fully remote. They are able to execute an entire M&A deal in a virtual setting.

One of the best things to do to encourage people to embrace tools is to show them how they will make their lives easier and their job less challenging. More often than not, if they understand the value that it brings, they will be willing to put more time into it.

This is also the experience of Naomi O'Brien when she was trying to implement tools when first joining Honeywell.

Implementing Tools in your team

"I got a lot of pushbacks in the beginning about standing up an M&A tool. People would often tell me that the tools are not perfect.

And I always agree that it's never going to be perfect, but what's important is that it's better. So, I always ask them:

- *Is it better than what we had?*

- *Is it enabling people to be more successful?*

- *Is it allowing efficiencies where you didn't have them?*

We had zero version control with Excel. But at least with a tool, you know it's real-time. People can go in and they can update their statuses.

You can see where things are at quickly, and visually, and you know where the issues and risks lie. There's a lot of value to be had there.

> *So articulating how this helps and improves their lives, really goes a long way."*
>
> **— Naomi O'Brien, Head of M&A Integration at Honeywell**

Below are just some of the technology tools that we recommend for a more efficient workflow.

Deal Management Software

The majority of organizations today are still using Excel spreadsheets to manage their entire deal. While that is viable, it's no longer the best option, since it lacks collaboration and transparency.

By using Excel trackers, there is a very linear workflow. One person sends the document to another team for updating. Then you have to wait for that updated version to be sent to another team member before they can start working there. Imagine ten or more team members using it at the same time. M&A teams need an M&A lifecycle management platform designed for collaboration and responsiveness.

We recommend using DealRoom because the platform makes M&A efficient by enabling cross-functional teams to collaborate in one place across the deal lifecycle. DealRoom prevents endless email threads and countless hours of updating the excel trackers.

The platform also has a built-in data room that allows users to manage workflows and sensitive data in one place. Having documents and information scattered all over can be chaotic. Files can get lost and overlooked in a complex environment.

Chat Tools

Having a dedicated chat tool for M&A deals is very beneficial. Chat tools promote transparency and collaboration for team members across the board. Having one place where all conversation happens also makes previous conversations available for anyone who wants to back-read.

We recommend using Slack. The tool gives teams multiple channels for different work streams, so information is not lost. You can have a separate channel for marketing, HR, diligence, or any other function, depending on your preferences.

Video Conferencing Platform

If you have international team members or want a more accessible cadence of meetings, video calls are the way to go. It allows for a more intimate conversation, even if you are not in the same room.

We recommend Zoom or Google Meet. Zoom is one of the most popular video-conferencing platforms in the world. It's very easy to use and offers free usage, albeit limited to 40 minutes per call. Google Meet is also another free-to-use platform that has no limit on your calls. If everyone is using Google accounts, Google Meet is the best option.

eSignature Software or Services

Another tool that helps finish work streams remotely is PDF readers, which allows for remote document signing. Each team member should be knowledgeable on how to use a tool like this, and Adobe Acrobat and DocuSign are the more popular choices in this area.

3rd Party Transactional Data Sets

3rd party transactional data sets are available and extremely helpful in sourcing companies. These tools provide access to financial information and org charts that are not available on public sites. Utilize 3rd part transactional sites to gauge whether or not the target is attractive before approaching them.

PitchBook and S&P Capital IQ are two of the most popular tools in the M&A world when it comes to gathering company information.

Satellite Imagery

With current fast-evolving technology, high-resolution aerial imagery is now a very reliable, possible option. It will improve due diligence and enable you to assess properties without leaving the office, saving valuable time in the process.

Satellite imagery can improve site evaluations by providing complete visual access to a property, the geographical locations, measurement of the property, the distance to the nearest competitor, etc.

Section 3.3: Documenting your Deals

Non-Disclosure Agreements

DEAL LEAD

A non-disclosure agreement is the first legal document to enter into with a seller. One of the biggest mistakes you can make is thinking that this is a routine exercise that you need to do just to get more information out of the target. An NDA is an important milestone that will set the stage for how you, the buyer, will be working with the seller moving forward.

Importance of NDA

"The most important thing to me in negotiating an NDA is to remember that this is not a random piece of legalese that the lawyers are going to talk on the side, and it's just a checkmark that by policy, both companies need to go through and carry on.

This is a fundamental piece of an M&A process that fulfills two critical things:

One, it establishes trust between the parties. It plays the framework for how the negotiation will be carried on throughout the diligence. And then, if this gets to the closing documents.

- *How will the parties work with each other?*

- *How will the commercial terms be discussed?*

- *How will the legal teams work with each other?*

- *Who has the balance of power?*

- *Who is flexible and who is not?*

- *Who has the decision authority?*

- *Do you need to go three levels up for every minor decision to be made or is the person on the phone actually allowed to make legal and business calls on the terms that are being negotiated?*

So, it really sets the tone for, um, the process going forward.

— **Mark Khavkin, CFO at Pantheon Platform.**

Trust is the most important element of negotiating an NDA. The last thing you want to do is win the negotiations but lose the deal entirely. Get into the mindset that having amicable negotiations is in your best interest.

NDA documents can be pretty standard. Many people like to use templates. However, as mentioned previously, take NDAs seriously since they can result in unlimited liabilities if breached. It is very easy to violate a contract that you did not fully understand. You might incur unnecessary restrictions and responsibilities if you don't negotiate properly. Here are a few things to watch out for:

Commitment to Closing

There needs to be a clear disclaimer on the NDA that just because the document is signed, doesn't mean that the deal is closed. If not, you could end up in litigation.

NDA ended up in Litigation

"You want a clear and conspicuous disclaimer on the NDA that says, just because we signed this document, doesn't mean we have a deal. It is the beginning of the deal, and your legal team should be able to provide that language for you.

We have seen a case law where an NDA doesn't have the right type of language, or the language goes beyond the confines of an NDA and talks about a partnership and a longstanding relationship. And that has gone to litigation where one-party claims that they have a deal.

So, you want to avoid that gray zone and get rid of any ambiguity and have that conspicuous language."

— Andrew Gratz, Associate General Counsel at LyondellBasell

One-way Restrictions

There are sellers that like to do one-way NDAs, where the buyer is the only party bound by confidentiality. However, it's wrong to think that the seller is the only one that needs protection. You, as the buyer, will also be disclosing confidential information to the target company as you go deeper into the transaction: such as your plans for their business, your process, technology, and the price.

You don't want the target company telling people that you're trying to buy their company for whatever reason and how much you would be willing to pay for their business. It could also attract potential competitors, which could increase the potential purchase price.

Unfair Duration

The target company can be too restrictive about the duration of confidentiality for obvious reasons. However, no one should be assuming indefinite liability for any data gathered during diligence.

According to Mark Khavkin, CFO at Pantheon Platform, three years are the common durations, and five years are the more exceptional ones, depending on the rationale. Any longer than that would be unfair, and you should avoid making such commitments.

Definition of Confidential Information

This is a very important aspect of the negotiations. Both parties must clearly define the scope of confidentiality.

First and foremost, you may have already acquired a good amount of information before you approach a target company. This includes information from their sales pitch deck, respective clients, prospects, analysts, and former employees. These are the things you gathered outside of the NDA and shouldn't be confidential.

Furthermore, both parties should clearly define what constitutes confidential information. Are they the ones that are verbally disclosed? Are they the ones in writing? Or are they the ones that are explicitly getting marked as confidential?

Finally, discuss the ramifications, if the deal falls apart. Do you have to destroy the information? Do you have to return it? Do you have to keep it? Clarify these things inside the NDA.

Non-Solicit or Non-Hires

Non-solicit or non-hires is something that the seller normally includes in their preferred NDA. It includes everything that you, as the buyer, cannot do with the people you encounter in the seller's company.

This is completely subjective and totally up to you, as the buyer, if you want to commit to it. However, it is important for you to know if this clause exists, so that you do not get blindsided when the deal doesn't go through.

For instance, let's say you are in a very small, niche industry and are looking to acquire a company in the same industry. If the deal falls apart, you will be cutting a huge part of your hiring potential, since you can no longer hire their employees for a substantial amount of time.

It is also important to draw boundaries to this clause. The very nature of this document binds the people involved in the deal to confident-iality. Therefore, what happens when someone outside the deal team, in good faith, recruits a friend inside the target company? Are you going to be held liable for that?

Finally, this clause should also be bilateral and should prevent the seller from recruiting the acquirer's employees.

Residual Memory Clause

If applicable in your deal, this is probably the most difficult part of the negotiations. The residual memory clause is a protection for the acquirer from any liability regarding the retained knowledge and information that they might have learned and retained during the entire M&A deal.

From a seller's perspective, it is in their best interest to not allow this clause, especially if their information or process is very sensitive and susceptible to imitation. However, from a buyer's perspective, if their process is ground-breaking and unique, it should have been patented in the first place.

As a compromise, both parties should meet in the middle and allow this clause. However, it should only be done on the premise that there would be no deliberate attempt to memorize the solution — no notes, pictures, reports, documentation, or any other form of extraction.

External Parties

As an acquirer, it is very common to hire external parties to assist in the transaction. Always remember that the same restrictions agreed upon in the NDA also apply to the external parties. This is why it is very important that each and every person involved in the transaction has a complete understanding of the NDA.

Preliminary Due Diligence

Diligence List

DEAL LEAD

The primary goal of preliminary due diligence is to identify whether this deal is right for you or not. The faster you get to that answer, the better. Most companies make the mistake of throwing 200 questions at the target, which would inevitably turn them off or burden them while trying to run the company. Optimize the diligence questions and make your list as short as possible.

Preliminary Due Diligence List:

"In my experience, owners usually worry that a deal can be taxing on their business and their employees. Especially when they don't have to tell everyone.

If you can reduce the number of questions that you need to get to an LOI, even if they are just a range of numbers, that is going to remove a huge obstacle and will allow you to close more deals. Simplify it to the bare minimum of what you need to get to an LOI."

— *Cameron Weiner, VP of Strategic Development, Head of M&A at Shopko Optical.*

Every company will have its own set of preliminary due diligence lists, depending on the types of deals that they want to do and what matters to them. However, there are a few sets of questions that are required in order to build a proper valuation of the target business for the LOI draft.

Below is an illustration of the preliminary due diligence list, together with what it would look like as it progressed to the confirmatory diligence phase.

Preliminary Due Diligence (sampling)	Confirmatory Due Diligence (sampling)
General Review	
Have there been any material acquisitions or dispositions over the past 5 years?	• Please provide all agreements and other documents related to all proposed or consummated mergers, acquisitions, or divestitures of assets and reorganizations and restructurings • Please provide any and all fictitious, assumed, or other business or trade names under which the Company and each of its subsidiaries are conducting or have conducted business
Latest capitalization table of the company. (# of shares, ownership percentages, etc.)	• Please provide a detailed capitalization (cap) table with all types of securities including options. Include a vesting schedule. • Please provide any and all agreements between the Company and any of its affiliates, officers, directors, employees, security holders or debt holders, or any entity controlled thereby or in which any has a financial interest • Please provide contracts and other documentation related to the sale, issuance, and terms of all the Company's equity and debt securities
Corporate structure - including a discussion of the business	• Please provide copies of offering memos prepared for or delivered

activities of any related entities.	to actual or potential purchasers of the Company's securities • Please provide any contracts issuing powers of attorney • Please send contracts and a history of conversations related to all proposed or consummated joint ventures, strategic alliances, partnerships, investments, or similar arrangements or relationships
What is your average sales price/deal size?	• Please provide quarterly sales, units, product cost, and product margin by customer, for the last 3 years and the current YTD period.
How long are your average customer contracts?	• To the extent not provided in response to any of the items elsewhere, please attach copies of significant customer sales contracts and accounting policy used for long-term contracts. Include any minimum quantity specifications and pricing terms.
Who are your largest competitors for each of your products?	• The same document from Preliminary Due Diligence can be reused for Confirmatory Due Diligence. In some cases, a more detailed market analysis can be provided by the Seller if the Seller has the time to do it. Otherwise, an investment banker or other service can be contracted by the Buyer to perform a similar analysis if more detail is needed. Pragmatically, the Buyer will perform this analysis already then

	anything provided by the Seller is validation of their common assumptions.
When you win a competitive sales process, why do you win? When you lose, why do you lose?	• Please attach descriptions of all trade secrets and other proprietary information material creating a competitive advantage
Where is your development team located? Do you outsource any development work or use any contractors?	• Please send an anonymized organizational chart by site indicating job titles/roles, functions/departments, and total numbers of employees within each function. Contractors can be listed also with their designation of FTE or PTE.
Where do you see your products fitting into our company? Where do you see potential synergies? Would your customer be interested in purchasing our product?	• A thoughtful and thorough response will be provided normally during Preliminary Due Diligence that can then be passed onto Confirmatory Due Diligence.
How do you foresee your offerings growing in the industry?	• Send growth retention and net retention rates for each of your products.
B. Financial Review	
Income statement and balance sheet for 3 years with segmentation by subsidiary and on a consolidated basis.	• Please send audited annual financial statements for the last 3 years • Please provide a file of annual expenses broken out by R&D, S&M, and G&A by material spend category
Quarterly projected income	• Please send a quarterly schedule

statement and additional years if available.	of cash and investments by category for the last year ended, the current YTD period, and the most recent month end • Please send a quarterly schedule of receivables by category for the last year ended and the current YTD period.
Quarterly historical projected revenue summary by revenue type, product, and region.	• Please send quarterly sales, units, product cost, and product margin by customer for the last 3 years and the current YTD period. • Please deliver a summary of special discounts and credit terms offered to customers. • To the extent not provided in response to any of the items elsewhere, please attach copies of significant customer sales contracts and accounting policy used for long-term contracts. Include any minimum quantity specifications and pricing terms.
C. Sales and Marketing	

List of your products and services with descriptions.	• Deliver an overview of products and services that are revenue generating
	  o Please provide a detailed description of modules and technologies.
	  o Any technical specifications are greatly appreciated
	Please provide standard product and service warranties issued to buyers or users of your products and services.

How many customers do you have? What is your breakdown of revenue by customer? What is your primary go-to-market?	• A thoughtful and thorough response will be provided normally during Preliminary Due Diligence that can then be passed onto Confirmatory Due Diligence. Whereby the Buyer wants more details than the Seller will use the same format from Preliminary Due Diligence, then expand on details needed by the Buyer such as a quarterly breakdown or a revenue forecast.
How do you sell? Do you have any partners in sales and marketing?	• Describe any and all relationships and commitments between the Company and external parties with whom information is exchanged. This includes suppliers, vendors, e-business partners, outsourced manufacturers, external consultants, etc. If collaboration activities exist with external parties, how is information exchanged? Is remote access to the company network provided to any external parties for purposes of collaboration? • Please attach all agreements and other documents related to all proposed or consummated strategic alliances, partnerships, joint ventures or similar arrangements

D. Human resources	
Org chart and headcount by function	• Attach an organizational diagram showing the current legal entity structure of the Company, including subsidiaries, if any. • Complete the attached Employee Data Template for all of the Company's employees
Have there been any layoffs or material changes to the workforce in the last 24 months?	• Send a list of the Company's former directors, officers, and key employees (noting job titles/roles, not names) that left the Company within the last 5 years, a description of the circumstances in which each left, and redacted copies of separation or resignation agreements, releases, and other related documentation (if any). • Please provide details of any prior, pending or threatened claims, audits or litigation, court or administrative proceedings or orders, regarding employment, benefits, unemployment, immigration, grievances, arbitrations, unfair labor practices, DOL notices, EEOC actions, WARN and ADA disputes or claims existing during the last 5 years (including worker compensation and disability claims)

Valuation

Most teams build their valuation model purely based on financial numbers. This is a mistake, since everything about the company affects the valuation. This is why teams should always work together and communicate constantly throughout the diligence process.

- Is the seller leaving post-close?
- Do they still want to stay and grow the business?
- Are key employees locked in, or can they leave anytime they want?

All of these things will and should impact the valuation of a business, depending on the deal rationale.

Most deal teams create their deal structure purely based on negotiations. They just try to get the best terms possible. However, this should not be the case. Integration should always be at the forefront of decision-making.

All of these things are connected: valuation, integration, and strategy. The valuation model is an output of integration planning, strategy, and diligence.

A Rigorous Valuation Methodology

"At the end of the day, the valuation that your financial model produces is an output, but the inputs, diligence, and integration planning, in many ways, are much more important. More often than not, bad deals happen because either the due diligence wasn't thorough, or the integration plan wasn't detailed enough or wasn't followed. Having a rigorous evaluation methodology keeps you honest and ensures that you're looking at not only the quantum but also the timing of synergies and the performance of the base business."

— Erik Levy, Group Head Corp Dev, and M&A at DMGT PLC

Carlos Cesta also backs this up with what he calls the three dials of a deal. The deal structure, risk management, and integration are all synced together. If you alter one of them, it affects the other two.

Three Dials of the Deal

"There are three dials of a deal. The first dial is the deal structure. How much are you paying? How do you break that down into different components? What you're trying to do is figure out how much cash upfront versus contingent payment to provide an opportunity to give upside to management if management overlaps with the shareholders.

Then you have the risk management part of the equation, which is the second dial of the deal. If you ask your risk guy, he's always going to say, put everything on contingent payment, nothing is fixed. So that's the extreme. Risk management is always going to push towards variable payment or if you find some uncertainty about the forecast in the deal.

And the third dial, which for me is the most important, is integration. Because the other two factors are going to interfere with how you integrate the company. And that's the one where I think you cannot compromise. What do I mean by that?

If there's no contingent payment or ability to incentivize management with the purchase price, then you're probably going to have to put some

sort of overlaying bonus in there to increase our chances to make more money into the deal, and guess what? That increases the overall price of the deal.

And also, conversely, this is the infamous part of the earnout. When you put a structure on the deal and you're still measuring the target profit after you've done the deal, it means that you have to keep that entity separate. It means that you cannot completely act like one company.

So for me, those are the three dials. And it's a fine balance between that. Once you turn the dial too much to one side, you mess up the other."

**— Carlos Cesta, Vice President,
Corporate Development/M&A at Presidio**

There are also companies, like AMN Healthcare, that have created a consolidated function that they call the Diligence and Integration Management Office (DIMO). In this function, 90% of their people in diligence are also part of the integration team. This limits the knowledge chasm between the two teams, since the integration team is already involved in the deal before the NDA is even signed.

Having this centralized function has helped them evolve their practice and become more efficient at integrating acquired companies.

Establishing the DIMO

"Traditionally the integration management office starts a couple of weeks before closing. They are really focused on integrating the business. But we saw through experience the importance of getting upfront, early, and thorough diligence. So, we felt like combining diligence and integration and having continuity, make a lot of sense.

If you want repeatability and scalability in your integration, you need somebody who is dedicated, who can pick up the learnings from integration to integration, from diligence to diligence, and be able to refine that process.

From a diligence standpoint, there are a lot of things that happen out there that don't make it into the diligence memo.

Those little things that you pick up in a hallway conversation, or during lunch when you're talking with the other management team, it helps with continuity and is really important for both the new company and your internal team members.

It also helps to eliminate redundancy and helps you become more efficient when you get to the integration."

— Kerry Perez, Head of Diligence and Integration Management Office (M&A) at AMN Healthcare

---

This is why you need a clear vision of your end state before going any further. Knowing what the end goal is and how you plan on integrating the company post-close will determine a lot of things, including the valuation model. From that end state, you can now start working your way backward until you can see a clear integration plan.

Developing the End State and Working Backwards

"When you're navigating, and you start to a point where you are one degree off from your desired state, over time, you become further and further away from your target. If you don't start with the end state and work backward, your navigation is going to be all wrong.

So, once we understand what the agreed-upon end state is that's really driving the value for the deal, then we start working through the gates coming back to the beginning. And the "how" is really the precursor to developing the end state and working backward.

How do they sell? How do they develop? How do they manage people? The how and the why is more important than the what.

We've got a model that says generate this much revenue. But how do we get to that number? Show me the math that gets to that number. And then, what are the costs associated with getting to that number?

And you can keep double-clicking like on a Google search, until you get to the end or till you get to the level of depth that gives you enough to move forward, to start building your plan."

— Jim Buckley, Vice President, Mergers and Acquisitions Integration at VMware

---

Letter of Intent

DEAL LEAD

As the acquirer, it is in your best interest to get to exclusivity as fast as possible. This is what an LOI is for. It is a formal letter to express a desire to purchase the company, which includes the price, exclusivity period, and the duration of the confirmatory diligence.

If you are in a bilateral deal with a good standing relationship with the target company, you can probably take your time and make sure this is the right deal for you before you sign an LOI. But if you are in a competitive process, all bets are off. You have to find a way to get to LOI, as fast as possible, especially if you are dealing with bankers.

How Banker's Processes Have Evolved

"The greatest risk to deals is time. So, we (bankers) have no interest in long exclusivity periods because we lose leverage.

If I grant a corporate buyer three weeks of exclusivity, I can't talk to any other buyers during that time. They can work through it and potentially decide that this is not the deal for them.

Then I have what's almost like a broken process and I have to go back groveling to my old buyers and ask to re-engage. That is no position to be in. We're also trying to avoid that at all costs.

It's not so much about having the timeline be as short as possible, but to have it as tight and efficient as possible.

If in the past we were taking ten or nine buyers post LOI and having a very competitive auction, now maybe we'll take five and have more focused time with them.

We think that there's a very high likelihood that one of them produces a great outcome for our clients. It reduces the extra work for those extra 4 or 5 that probably aren't going to be your winner anyway.

We're going to push all of these guys as hard as we can. There's going to be some natural fallout so that three of them are basically ready to sign a deal days after they submit their package. That's our focus.

It's not necessarily about value maximization. It's about deal certainty. However, in these competitive businesses, the market and the competition drive value maximization.

Our role is to get great deals and optionality for our clients that creates deal certainty. That's my obligation to my client, it's not value maximization."

— Kunal Jain, Vice President, Corporate Development & Strategy at GCX Mounting Solutions

However, as corporate development, make sure that the business will do the diligence when you sign an LOI. Otherwise, you can damage your brand in the market.

As discussed earlier in this book, you need to shorten your preliminary due diligence to the core questions and concerns, in order to make the process faster and more efficient.

CEO

One of the best things to do is give the head of corporate development or the business unit authority to sign an LOI. This will shorten the overall process and will allow you to compete in a competitive process. Losing a deal because you were too slow in signing an LOI is painful.

Section 3.4: Negotiating the Deal

We have often seen where poor negotiations led to breaking the deal altogether, or worse, a catastrophic integration. This happens when a party refuses to compromise and has a very negative approach to the negotiations.

DEAL LEAD

The best deals are the ones where both parties walk away happy. As a good negotiator, draw the line on the areas that you can't budge because they are vital to the strategy. However, in the other areas where you can, try to make the other party feel good about the deal. These folks are going to be critical for the business post-close.

Relationships With the Seller

"In order to have a successful negotiation as a corporate development professional, there's a lot of relationships all day. You have to keep in mind that it's not just about winning the negotiation at all costs for Microsoft. Obviously, my job is to do the best deal for Microsoft but remember that the company and the people in it are going to become a part of Microsoft. I'm negotiating with somebody who is eventually going to be on my team.

The relationship you build with that person and making sure that you're building a transaction and an outcome that is good, not only for Microsoft but everyone such that you're going to have a happy, productive, and successful team of people that come into Microsoft, adds a layer of complexity that I enjoy."

— Devorah Bertucci, VP, Corporate Development at Netflix

Winning on every point will only make you feel good at the moment. However, it could harm the overall business goal that you're trying to achieve.

According to Larry Forman, Senior Manager at Deloitte, there are three key pillars to effective M&A negotiations:

1. **Be fair** — Try to find a middle ground because most M&A negotiations are not one-and-done. A long-term relationship is important because there will be further negotiations down the line, and you will most likely be working together post-close.

2. **Be open and honest** — Trust is extremely valuable when it comes to negotiations. Give context to what you're trying to do and why you are negotiating for specific items. The other party will most likely be amicable if they understand you.

3. **Be empathetic** — As you understand the situation and the rationale of the other party, be empathetic to their situation. The goal is to satisfy both parties. After securing the right mindset and approach, let's talk about some of the most highly negotiated parts of the deal.

4. **Letter of Intent** — One of the most commonly negotiated parts of an LOI is the price and exclusivity period. You can offer a price range and explain what it would take for you to pay the highest number, the value detractors that will pull you down in the middle number, and eventually the lowest number.

When it comes to exclusivity, the seller will always be hesitant to give long exclusivity. Explain what will cause delays in the deal, for instance, your pre-close conditions. If they understand you, they will more likely agree to your proposal.

There are also instances where the seller doesn't have automatic assignment clauses in their customer contracts. If this is vital in your deal rationale, then you have to declare it as a pre-closing condition. This alone can be a deal stopper and should be negotiated upfront.

5. **Sensitive Information** — While there is a lot of sensitive information in an M&A transaction, negotiating around sensitive information happens a lot in a technology sale. These are commonly the codes or intellectual property that make the company special, which is why the target doesn't want to expose it, until they are certain that the deal will go through. There are a couple of ways that you can deal with this.

    The first one is to break down the diligence into two parts. Proceed with everything else, except the sensitive information. Towards the end, when the deal is more likely to close, you can do final diligence on the sensitive information.

    If the seller still refuses, you can hire a third party to perform the diligence for that particularly sensitive information. That way, you are not exposed to it, even if the deal breaks down.

6. **Automatic Assignments** — As stated above, this is highly negotiated, depending on your demands. If the seller's contracts don't have automatic assignment clauses and you need to secure clients before closing the deal, you need to approach them without violating the NDA agreement.

    Have the seller approach their clients and inform them of the sale towards the end of the process. This is a subtle way to get the seller's permission to involve other parties outside of the NDA and the client's permission to involve you in their agreement.

7. **Retention Bonuses** — If retaining key employees is crucial to a transaction, then golden handcuffs are another area to negotiate. There are a couple of ways to go about this. Hopefully, by this stage, you have already explained to the seller the deal rationale.

Even though closing the deal already incentivizes the seller, you can offer additional bonuses if they help you get commitment from key employees. Stay bonuses are also pretty common in these kinds of scenarios. You can only access a sum amount of money that you pool together for the employees who stay for a specific amount of time. Whether you or the seller pays for these golden handcuffs is highly negotiated.

8. **Disclosure schedules** — This document defines the parameter of the transaction. It is important to prepare this as early as possible, so the business sponsor can personally review the schedules. Do not pawn it off for the lawyers alone to review.

   The business sponsor and the financial people have to be the ones to review this because no one knows the business more than they do. They will know what should and should not be included in the sale. If the lawyers are the only ones reviewing this, you will only get a legal point of view of the document.

9. **Limitations of liability** — There are instances where the seller doesn't own their IP, and they're trying to sell it. Negotiate for unlimited liability in this case, since you have a high risk of exposure.

10. The limitations of liability are typically limited and agreed upon by both parties. What you should negotiate is the amount to be put in a holdback. This means that you will put a certain amount of the purchase price in an escrow and hold it there for a certain period of time. If nothing unexpected occurs, then the seller will receive the money.

11. **Non-compete** –Negotiating the duration of this part is pretty common. Unless the seller intends to sell you the business and quickly battle you in the market, there is no reason to dwell on the

non-compete. Two to three years are the typical time range, and five years for special cases. However, anything more than five years is too much, and you should not agree to anything more than five years.

12. It's important to note that if you are a large company that is divesting a business unit, watch out for the buyer's definition of your business. There are instances where the buyer might define your business too broadly in the non-compete section so that it might hinder your parent company's operations.

Section 3.5: Confirmatory Diligence

DEAL LEAD

As the name suggests, this phase is about confirming what you're buying. At this stage, you now have access to all kinds of documents necessary to understand the entire business pre-acquisition. The questions you had from the preliminary due diligence will now go deeper and wider as you prepare to acquire the company. This is where to confirm if your initial integration thesis, or end state, is still viable and aligned with the strategy.

Preliminary Due Diligence	Confirmatory Due Diligence
1. Balance Sheet	Income statements Accounts payable Accounts receivable Tax returns
2. Customer list	Customer contracts Contact numbers
3. Org Chart	Job title Salary Employment contract
4. Product Information	Patent Design Product Recalls

Selecting your Integration Lead

This is also where integration planning should start. Selecting the right integration lead is a must. The primary role of the integration lead is to achieve the right value for your acquisitions. Here there are two options: hire an external person or select someone from the business line.

It may not always be possible, but the integration lead should come from the business that will inherit the acquired company post-acquisition. No one knows the business better than they do, so it would be wise for them to lead the integration planning and execution.

Ideal Integration Leader

"The best possible person to become an integration leader actually comes from the business line, more than it comes from somebody who's in the enterprise PMO.

To be a project manager, there's a lot of rigor that you go through to become a certified project manager. What I found in other project managers that I've worked with is that they have a very linear perspective of how to run their approach for a project.

While I appreciate all that because I love to have somebody on my team who can do what they do and they're really good at it. Sometimes, they are so focused on delivering the outcomes of that one project, they don't look above and beyond the implications of a particular issue or risk.

They can learn all that, but it takes time and maturity.

On the other hand, when you have somebody from the business line, this individual already also has the expanse of communication and network with other business line lines.

They know the business, they know the key people inside the business that they can work with, and they have credibility."

— John Morada, COO at M&A Science

According to John Morada, these are the top three attributes to look for in an integration leader:

1. **Organized** — This role has a variety of responsibilities across different workstreams, so the integration leader needs to be skilled at organization and prioritization.

2. **High emotional intelligence** — You need someone who knows how to listen to and empathize with people. This person needs to show great leadership skills to manage all the workstreams.

3. **Critical thinking** — It is crucial that the integration leader knows how to look at problems, find the critical items that are causing them, and have the ability to find solutions to those problems.

4. **Strong Communication** — This person needs to be able to communicate the importance of integration to the process and be able to collaborate well with all the teams that are necessary to complete the integration.

Prioritizing Deliverables

As previously mentioned, most companies tend to rely too much on checklists. In fact, some people don't look outside the checklists. They believe that their checklists will have everything they need to do the deal successfully. Even if that were true, throwing 500 questions all at once to the seller will not yield the best results.

The reality is that every deal is different. Not all of those questions will apply to a particular seller or a particular industry. It also wouldn't be an efficient use of time, since you will be waiting for the seller to finish that checklist before you can move forward. **Dissecting your checklist into separate phases is the best way to go about the process.**

Furthermore, you don't want to distract the seller from running the business that you are trying to acquire. Making the diligence process more efficient is crucial to success since it will save time and money. According to James Harris, here's how you can do it:

Question	Status	Priority	Location
Financial Statements	Resolved	High	HTML Link
HR Contracts	In-Progress	Medium	
Accounts Payable	Open	Low	
Product Recalls	N/A	-	-
Lease Contracts	N/A	-	-

- First Phase — Head of Corp Dev, CEO, and Deal Sponsor should take a pass at the diligence list and mark the level of priorities based on the deal rationale. If there are non-applicable questions, they should label them, so no one wastes their time on them.

  For instance, if you are buying a business that hasn't released a product yet, then questions regarding product recall and warranties should not apply to that transaction.

  Any file uploaded in the data room should be easy to locate. Putting that location category in your diligence list will help you save time and avoid "treasure hunting" when you reach hundreds of files.

- Second Phase — Now that you have decided that the target is worth buying, you can then proceed to the next phase of your diligence checklist, which is a deeper understanding of how to integrate the target into your company.

At this time, you will now be bringing in functional teams to help with the diligence process. Set up a meeting with your team, and make sure they all understand the deal rationale. If they don't understand the deal rationale, they will not be able to ask intelligent questions and prepare the integration plan properly.

Give them access to the checklist and have them filter that list according to priorities. Make sure they also understand how to use the checklist to avoid redundancies and misplacing files after uploads.

- Third Phase — Now that the checklist is completely optimized, share it with the inbound CEO. Explain to them that you need the high priorities first, and they can also mark the non-applicable ones as soon as possible.

Due Diligence Team

DEAL LEAD

When executing an entire deal, you will need many different types of functional experts in their respective fields. Not all transactions are the same, so getting all of them in-house is not a good idea. Hire external people to accomplish full diligence during this phase and borrow some internal people to work on the transaction.

According to Ben Sutton, Director, Corporate Development at Equifax, these are just some of the most common teams needed during the diligence process.

1. Legal Corporate Team

It is probably the most important team in during diligence. This team will consist of both outside advisors, who are doing most of the heavy lifting, and the internal legal team working on the critical issues of incorporating the business and whether or not they properly file the paperwork.

- Who owns the business?
- What is the capitalization of the business?
- Who was on the board of directors of the business?
- What are the minutes associated with the board meetings that gave the authority to sell the business?
- They are also looking for any past or present litigations.

Outside of diligence, this is also the team responsible for negotiating, drafting, and adjusting the purchase agreement and other legal documentation needed for the transaction.

2. Legal IP team

When applicable, this is the second most important legal team. Intellectual property is prevalent in the tech industry when the acquisition is about software solutions, and this team focuses on:

- Reviewing patents and trademarks.
- Looking at contractor and employment agreements for infringement and liabilities
- Foreign trademarks
- Customer agreements

The primary role of this team is to ensure that the seller has proper ownership of the intellectual property. If they do not, necessary amendments need to be made to the customer and vendor agreements to ensure that no one will have a claim on the intellectual property you're buying.

3. Legal Commercial Team

This team will work with the legal IP team in looking at the proper ownership of the intellectual property. However, their main role is more focused directly on the customers and vendor contracts.

They will assess the limitations of liabilities and the level of exposure of the seller in those contracts. They either get special protection in the purchase agreement or exclude that contract from the transaction itself.

4. Human Resources Team

This team will also work very closely with both internal and external employment lawyers. Their primary focus is on FLSA issues:

- Are the employees exempt or nonexempt?
- What's their compensation?
- How are employees being paid?
- Are they properly compensated?
- Has the business properly collected all immigration forms?
- Are all employees legally allowed to work?
- What are the benefits for the employees?
- How does it compare to the acquirer's benefits package, and how do you close the gap?

Aside from this, HR is very much involved in understanding the key talents. They will work closely with the management team of the target business to get a clear understanding of who does what and how to retain them. They are in charge of designing retention packages.

5. Accounting Due Diligence team

    Usually, you hire a third-party team to get a more detailed look at the financials. This team will look at direct invoices, customer contracts, vendor agreements, and employment agreements to ensure that the revenue and other financials are accurate.

    They also provide a quality-of-earnings report to understand how reliable and recurring those earnings are. They also work with the seller regarding the balance sheet requirements.

6. Tax Team

    Possibly from the same company where you hired the accounting team, the tax team is focused on the tax compliance of the seller. There could be misfiling that would expose the seller to penalties, and this team must identify and compute that, so the buyer can voluntarily pay for those taxes.

    This team will also work closely with HR and the legal team to look for any other tax associated with payroll and the most advantageous way to set up your corporate structure from a tax standpoint.

7. IT Team

    This team is to identify the tools the target company uses in their business. They will also need to understand what applications they are using and why. The IT team also has to look at cybersecurity. Has there been a breach, and how did they fix it?

8. Real Estate Team

    Assuming that the business is not fully remote, there will be offices, leased or owned. This team needs to review those leases and restrictions that might derail the deal. They could end up changing the lease or issuing a new one, assuming that the original lessor agrees.

If the seller owns the place, they could negotiate if the buyer wants to buy the infrastructure, rent it, or move all the employees to another location.

9. Insurance Team

Reviewing all the insurance policies of the target company will be the role of this team.

- Directors and Officers Insurance
- Errors and Omissions Insurance
- Cybersecurity Insurance

They need to make sure that the seller is adequately insured. If they're not, then this is something to negotiate in the purchase agreement.

10. Treasury Team

This team is in charge of the immediate cash issues associated with closing. When you're buying a business, you are inheriting a bank account that will be empty, and that will cause problems from a business continuity standpoint.

To keep the business going, they will have to work with the seller to understand the weekly or monthly cash needs, such as payroll and bills.

The treasury team will also oversee any liens that the buyer will inherit and any capital-raising effort that needs to happen to close the deal.

The size of the diligence team will depend on the deal size. It should consist of at least one to five internal people in each of these functional areas, including your M&A dedicated people. You should also hire a minimum of three external teams: A legal team, accounting team, and tax team.

It is also important to mention that you need to hire special consultants based on your needs. For instance, if you are reviewing a technology beyond your internal team's expertise, then hiring a specialist would be a great idea. There are also some things that the seller will only share with external parties for confidentiality reasons.

The last thing you want to do is under-resource the diligence team. Due to the exclusivity period stated in the LOI, you will most likely be working under time constraints. Therefore, you need this team to be optimally performing.

Internal Alignment

In a waterfall approach, every function working on the deal will have a set of checklists. Their only goal is to cross off items on the lists. It didn't matter if they were gathering useless information or if they were redundant. This can frustrate the buyer and waste time and resources.

In a goal-oriented model, like Agile, everyone needs to know what the acquisition strategy is, so they know what to look for. For every finding, they know if it's crucial to the deal because they educate themselves on the deal rationale. Before beginning the formal diligence process, we highly suggest that you conduct a kickoff meeting that would put everyone on the same page.

Play # 3 — Kickoff Meeting

❖ **Description:** Ensure that everyone involved in the M&A initiative shares a common understanding of the project and of their roles.

❖ **Author:** Kison Patel, CEO and founder of M&A Science

About the play

The entire program team (including all project team members) attends a kickoff meeting to encourage alignment.

Kickoff meetings can be used to launch various aspects of the M&A lifecycle but are most commonly associated with due diligence; the commencement of diligence is often a source of difficulty for many organizations.

The preliminary stages of the deal culminate in the kickoff, which marks the formalized intent to buy or sell a company and officially signals the deal leaving the drawing board. The kickoff is a critical moment for establishing the tone and momentum of the deal process in a larger sense. A well-planned and well-executed kickoff elevates the morale of the deal team and promotes confidence both internally and externally.

A botched kickoff can have the opposite effect, casting a shadow over the entire M&A project. On a more pragmatic level, teams leave good kickoff meetings informed, aligned, and with clarity regarding their roles, duties, and overarching end goals.

Accordingly, the kickoff plays a crucial role in enabling a team to operate in an Agile manner. At the broadest level, the kickoff meeting ensures that everyone involved in the M&A initiative shares a common understanding of the project and their roles.

Preparation

A note before you begin — especially if you're working with less experienced participants:

1. Explain the process, what types of people should be involved, and what they should do.

2. Then keep the conversation pretty high level so as not to lose people/overwhelm them. Describing the process at a high level essentially means focusing on things, such as the first three things they need to do right away and what they need to do before the first meeting.

People: The entire project team, including all contributors, consultants, sponsors, and team leads. The deal lead drives the kickoff meeting. Representatives from the Corporate Development team and the deal PM play supporting roles, as needed.

Difficulty: Moderate to Difficult

Materials: When it comes to materials for a kickoff meeting, tech tools are a critical topic of discussion. Selecting tech tools and choosing web-based collaborative software platforms can help teams realize the Agile goals of cross-functional visibility, collaborative workflow, and comprehensive information access. During due diligence, the choice of the data room will likely be out of the deal team's hands. However, the team can nevertheless establish internal project management and communication tools to use throughout the process. Using the same suite of tools in task tracking and communication throughout the entire M&A lifecycle alleviates many of the old headaches and obstacles associated with Excel and email and helps to transmit the information uncovered during due diligence over to the integration effort.

Time: 90 minutes

Running the Play

1. Overview of the target asset and strategy

   Questions to be considered here include who is the target, what business is the target in, where is the target located, and why is this target important (what is the strategy and value behind this target; how will this target help you meet your goals)?

Learning about the target will help you understand what it can/ cannot do well and tailor your process accordingly.

2. Name conditions for success

   What specific goals and benchmarks need to be set and realized in order for this endeavor to be considered successful?

3. Identify challenges & risks

   Name and discuss any challenges, risks, or concerns which have or have not already been identified.

4. Corporate Development presents other relevant information

   Additional relevant information includes, but is not limited to:

   - Milestones, roles, and duties for due diligence (that is, who needs to do what, and by when)
   - Milestones, roles, and duties for integration planning
   - Who can communicate with the target asset and under what circumstances
   - How the deal team works together (eg tools to use, communication styles, plays to run)

5. Establish a cadence for meetings

   Once you get a sense of how the other side works (and how quickly they work), you can establish a cadence for meetings, remembering to focus on meetings as needed, not meetings for the sake of meetings.

6. Additional tips & pointers for running a kickoff meeting:

- Scaling kickoff meetings: The kickoff meeting can be scaled down and run by small groups addressing sub-processes within a larger project. The small-scale kickoff is especially useful during post-merger integration when numerous small teams will be working on independent projects in parallel. Augmenting a team-wide integration kickoff meeting with smaller functional kickoffs allows alignment to simultaneously grow from both the bottom up and the top down.

- Anti-patterns to avoid: Information silos and/or bottlenecks, inefficient information management, "expert only" involvement in decision-making.

Cadence of Meetings

It is important that during in-flight, this team has constant communication with each other. There are many interdependencies in each functional area, and you need to promote transparency. For example, the legal team should also assess if HR discovers a problem in one of the employees' contracts. The tax team discovering misfilings would result in the acquiring company paying. Therefore, they should inform the accounting team and the legal team.

The Importance of Consistent Team Meetings

"You need to have constant communication between who has found what because there are many overlapping issues that can come from one functional area that needs to be known or can be addressed by another functional area.

Particularly when you remember the fact that we have the legal corporate team dealing with the purchase agreement itself. And they

---

> *are incorporating details from every single functional area, potentially based on what they found. So constant communication based on schedules is probably better.*
>
> *It also helps push people and actually review the materials because there is a lot of material in due diligence."*
>
> **— Ben Sutton, Director, Corporate Development at Equifax.**

Keeping consistent meetings will help people work faster and more efficiently. Hold meetings once or twice a week, or have more frequent meetings with the smaller teams, and then have the bigger team meet once a week.

Here's an Agile play that you can execute:

Play # 4 — Standup Meetings

❖ **Description** - Transfer essential business project knowledge and reduce risks. Allow transparency between departments. Resolve intra-team issues.

❖ **Author** - Kison Patel, CEO and founder of M&A Science

About the play

A team standup is essential for the transfer of essential knowledge, transparency, efficiency, and risk reduction. Team leads (project managers) must collaborate regularly to identify cross-team issues and risks.

For instance, each team works on their own projects. Standups allow transparency between departments and a time to communicate about any cross-departmental bottlenecks. We will take integration as an examplee.

All teams actively working on the integration project should hold standup meetings to maintain the internal and cross-functional alignment achieved during the integrated kickoff. Ultimately, the objective of this play is to enable all teams to communicate progress and obstacles, which, in turn, encourages efficient resolution of intra-team issues.

Preparation:

People: All team leads/project managers

Materials: None

Difficulty: Easy to Moderate

Time: While times may vary depending upon the number of team leads, it is best practice to set a time limit before the meeting starts, as well as a time limit for each team lead. Five minutes per team lead/project manager is a commonly used limit.

Running the Play

1. Establish schedule and location

   20 minutes pre-standup: Standups should follow a regular schedule and maintain a consistent location. During the height of a deal, these standups might take place multiple times a week (two or three max).

   Some expert practitioners feel Monday mornings are an ideal time to hold the standup. Moreover, since the deal team and their subteams overlap in membership, create a schedule of meetings in order to organize and coordinate standup participation.

2. Identify representatives from each team

   5 -10 minutes pre-standup: It is essential to include representatives from each team to ensure transparency and thorough communication.

3. Establish a protocol for escalation of critical issues

   10 - 15 minutes pre-standup: It is helpful to establish a facilitator to keep time and to intervene when conversations become heated.

   Some refer to this member of the standup as the "referee." In a similar vein, communicating clear standards of behavior and the importance of preparation for the meeting is essential when dealing with critical issues that will undoubtedly arise during a deal's lifecycle.

4. Clarify meeting goals and process flow

   Five minutes at the commencement of the standup: Having a clear goal and agenda keeps the meeting focused and avoids the common pitfall of meetings becoming unwieldy and unproductive.

5. Hold the meeting

   Time will vary: Again, a pre-established code of conduct, time limit, and expectations will all work to drive successful multi-team standups.

   Standups should incorporate what team members have worked on since the last standup, the plan for the day, and any roadblocks.

   To respect other members' time, if there are any one-off conversations you need to have with other team members, try to connect them after the meeting.

Integration-Led Confirmatory Due Diligence Process

There is another way to take Agile to a new level. According to **Jim Buckley, Vice President, Mergers and Acquisitions Integration at VMware,** another option is to have the integration lead run the confirmatory due diligence process.

The primary role of corporate development is to find and close deals. As soon as the deal closes, they are off to find the next best deal for the company. That is the very nature of the corporate development function. Therefore, they will hand off post-closing to the integration team.

Corporate Development vs. Integration Team

"Corp dev is literally transaction-led. They go from deal to deal to deal to deal, and that's what they should do. That's what they're supposed to do. They're always looking out for that next deal.

The integration team, it's a bit of a long trudge and you have to live with it. They drink all the Kool-Aid, they know what they're going to do, they know what the north star looks like, what creating value looks like, and if they have all the pieces to do everything else.

So, that's what the difference has been in my experience.

Corp dev typically will hand-off. Some even throw it over the wall. And you can lose a lot of the secret sauce from handoff to handoff to handoff.

**— Jim Buckley, Vice President,
Mergers and Acquisitions Integration at VMware**

On the other hand, the integration team's primary role is to create value out of transactions. Hence, they have different lines of questioning and mindsets, and will not leave until the integration is complete. These reasons make the integration team the better fit to lead the diligence process.

If you want to implement this process, involving the integration lead pre-LOI is a must. There should be zero hand-offs in this approach because the integration lead needs to hear the dialogue with the seller at the very beginning.

As you move towards the formal diligence process, have the integration lead ask the questions. They know all the right questions to ask that are necessary to create value from the transaction. During this phase, the integration team should act as the central hub that distributes all the findings to their respective functions.

For instance, the integration team should give all the valuation findings to corporate development, who is in charge of negotiating with the seller. They are also the ones who will provide the legal team with every document necessary for legal due diligence.

This process removes redundancies during questioning, preventing burnout from the sell-side that could harm the business. It will also give the integration team an early start on the integration planning.

Section 3.6: Integration Planning

DEAL LEAD

Probably the number one cause of deal failures is the knowledge chasm between the corp dev team and the integration team. We often see diligence and integration as a separate workstream. The integration team is involved after the deal is closed and they have zero knowledge of the deal or the company. As a result, they have to re-diligence the company all over again. This wastes time, money, and causes deal fatigue.

M&A is a Lot Like Buying a House:

"Once you've selected a place and put in your preliminary offer or your letter of intent, from there you move into the home inspection process, which is due diligence. Integration planning is just like planning to move into your new home. And you're probably going to do that at the same time as you're going through your home inspection. I know when I've purchased my home, I think about, okay, this is where I'll stick the

---

> *couch. I really don't like that paint color; I really want to do something different with that kitchen light. I'm already planning to move in, even before I've got the keys to the house at closing."*
>
> **— Klint Kendrick - Chairman | HR M&A Roundtable**

Planning integration alongside diligence also makes sense because every finding could have integration implications. Whether they're from an HR, legal, accounting, or even a leadership perspective, all of these implications can affect the overall integration process.

Bringing Integration Early in Diligence

"One of the biggest lessons that I learned on a couple of my first deals was we did not have that integration function attached at the hip with me from the minute we signed that letter of intent through the entire diligence process. That created challenges in having a more smooth integration process.

Involving an integration lead from very early in the diligence process is important because there are many things, we learn that can have integration implications. That visibility, early in the process and as we are building up the integration plan, makes us smarter across each of the functions."

— Jeremy Segal, Senior Vice President of Corporate Development at Progress

---

Play # 5 — Parallel Planning for Integration

❖ **Description** — Learn how to plan for integration during other stages of a deal's lifecycle.

❖ **Author** — Kison Patel, CEO and founder of M&A Science

About the play

When approaching a deal and assembling the teams involved, always remember: the earlier you bring the integration staff into a deal, the more likely the deal is to meet its ultimate objectives.

The integration lead's involvement ideally begins at the earliest strategic meetings, outlining the initiative itself, and extends through the conclusion of the M&A process. During the pre-close phase of the deal, the role of the integration lead is to

1. Provide a tactical perspective to the business development and deal teams.

2. Create a detailed post-merger integration plan to be executed on day one.

Preparation

People: Integration team, specifically the integration lead, due diligence team, Corporate Development, and other stakeholders

Materials: None

Difficulty: Moderate to Difficult

Time: 15 minutes

Running the Play

1. Select a strong integration lead

   An integration lead should have a robust business background (the more experience, the better), strong communication skills, and credibility.

2. Have Corporate Development include the integration lead during the targeting stage

    This helps Corporate Development have a stronger understanding of some of the integration criteria and considerations. It also empowers the integration team to perform better valuation, which can result in reduced risks.

3. Include the integration lead in diligence meetings. When possible, have members overlap both teams.

    When possible, having members of the diligence team also on the integration team is useful because information does not have to be transferred.

    Moreover, throughout the diligence process, the integration team members or lead can keep critical integration items in mind, such as go-to-market strategy and the integration of work streams and processes.

Another mistake is that people build their integration plan without the seller's input. Remember, no one knows the business more than the seller, and you need their perspective as to how the company should run post-close. Involve and create the integration plan with the CEO of the target company.

This is the perfect time to validate your synergies around the business and develop a go-to-market plan with the target CEO. Communicate your plans and the changes that will happen for them post-close. This includes what happens to their equipment, brand, employees, work structure, etc. Achieving alignment with the CEO of how the company will be run post-acquisition is paramount to your success.

Cisco's Strategy Session

"Before we close, our goal is to bring in the target leaders and have them sit down with our team, the business leaders, corp dev, or dev integration, and to have a strategy alignment session.

They know their business way better than we know it. We are making our best view of their business based on what we've learned and extrapolating, what does that mean inside of Cisco? How do we make that business successful inside of Cisco?

So, the more we can get their validation, allows us to get to that early alignment between the two companies, particularly around the product strategy and the go-to-market strategy, as well as the people.

It's really important to get that level of alignment between Cisco and the target company. And we feel the earlier we can do it, the better it sets us up for success."

— **Karen Ashley, Vice President, Corporate Development Integration at Cisco.**

Setting Success Metrics

DEAL LEAD

One of the biggest problems in integration is the lack of an agreed-upon measure of success. People often overlook this, which causes chaos in the organization post-close because they don't know if the acquisition was successful or not. Having a set of success metrics will also give team members a north star that they can strive for.

Document and establish measurements of success early on in the process. The measurements should be simple and unanimous because everyone needs to agree on what successful integration looks like. They should also be based on the value drivers of the deal, which derive from the strategic rationale.

How to Measure Success

"One of the biggest problems in integration is the lack of an agreed-upon measure of success.

If you are truly integrating something that's acquired, then determining its impact in isolation is inherently difficult. I'm going to merge all my systems. I'm going to merge my business processes. Then how do I determine the value of what I acquired when my goal is, in fact, to make it part of one unified organization.

So, in other words, your overarching goal works against measuring in isolation. And that's just a known M&A dilemma. But what you can do is to establish what those measures are going to be.

Make them as simple as possible. Make them directionally representative and then communicate it, so that everybody's on the same page.

They're never going to be perfect, but you know what it is, you know how to calculate, and we're agreed that that's what we're going to measure ourselves.

If you don't establish that upfront and it's every man for himself, we can all manipulate numbers to get to where we want to go."

— ***Mike Devita, Success Strategy Lead at Salesforce***

Here's how you can keep your success metrics simple:

Value Drivers	Success Metrics
Revenue	Did you hit your revenue numbers?
Employee Attrition	How many employees did you lose? It must be not more than 10% of the total population. You need to retain these people for X amount of time.

Key employees	Need to retain 100% of key employees
Customer Attrition	How many customers did you lose? It should not exceed more than X amount of the revenue.
Product Integration	Is the product that you acquired fully integrated and ready to go to market?

Just remember that these metrics that you set are only applicable if the deal rationale hasn't changed. If it changes materially, then these metrics will not be accurate anymore. Adjust them accordingly.

Changing Success Metrics

"If the strategy materially changes post-close, the deal is right out of the gate. Because the initial validation and reason that you went to the board to ask permission to spend a bunch of money, has fundamentally changed.

So, this is basically a new deal. If you think about the way the process works, it's effectively a new deal. It's a new project at a minimum.

— Jim Buckley, Vice President, Mergers and Acquisitions Integration at VMware

Focus on Employee Retention

HR LEAD

Losing key people post-close is the biggest value leak in a transaction. Unless you are buying intellectual property or removing people as part of your strategy or synergy, retaining people in the acquired business is in your best interest.

The first step to planning employee retention is to identify the key people that you absolutely need to retain that are crucial in the operation of the business post-close. Even with every intention to retain key employees, professionals can fail to identify those key people due to a lack of communication. Communication and a regular cadence of meetings are absolutely critical in the M&A process. Klint Kendrick has a fascinating story of his first time leading a deal:

A Story of Overlooking a Key Employee

"I had a couple of deals. I'd been acquired a few times. I had a pretty good idea of how it works, and it was my turn to step up to the front.

We acquired this company, and I was doing my victory lap. We're really excited. We got through the announcement meeting. And then we came back the next day, and one of the most critical technical employees was pissed.

He felt like he had been devalued in this process because he hadn't received a retention agreement. He'd never even come to my attention as the HR guy on the deal. And part of that was because I hadn't taken the time to reach out to some of my peers in our other functions."

— *Klint Kendrick, HR M&A Leader with several Fortune 500 firms*

Because of this unfortunate event, Klint made sure he never committed the same mistake twice. He developed a play that he likes to call the Post-Diligence Huddle.

Play # 6 — Identify Key People and Roles for Retention

❖ Description: Use this play to determine which roles you want to retain.

❖ Author: Klint Kendrick, HR M&A Leader with several Fortune 500 firms.

About the play

The premature exit of key employees can significantly affect both integration plans and the ongoing operation of the combined business. In many cases, an exodus of certain critical team members can destroy deal value.

Because of this effect on the success of the transaction, one of the most important steps to ensure retention is understanding how likely it is that a key employee will choose to leave.

Use this play to determine which roles you want to retain. This play provides a rough measure of the likelihood that a critical incumbent will leave for a different opportunity. The appropriate members of the deal team should come together for the discussion, allowing enough time to discuss each employee's individual situation.

Preparation:

People: HR, Corporate Development, Business Sponsor, Diligence Team

Difficulty: Medium

Materials: Paper and pen, employee census, org chart, good judgment

Time: 2+ hours

Running the Play:

1. Review Key Employees

   Working with your critical stakeholders, create a list of those employees who are known to be key to

   - the integration and
   - ongoing operations

During the diligence phase, notice employee names that arise during conversations. They should include:

- Employee listed in the CIM.

- Employees called out on the target website.

- Employees on succession plans.

- Employees in leadership development programs

- Employees noted as 'high potentials'

- Employees who have received significant compensation increases, bonuses, equity, etc. in the past three years.

2. Review Key Roles

Using the preliminary integration plan, understand which work should be done by an employee at the target company.

For example, if novating supplier agreements is a significant part of the deal, the supplier management leader should be on the list. Look for any roles that should be part of the retention discussions and add them to the list generated in step one.

3. Use the Post-Diligence Huddle to Gather Any Other Names

Use the post-diligence huddle to determine if anybody critical to the integration of operations is missing using the reviews above. Each function should create a list of critical people for consideration in this process.

4. Determine How Important Each Role is to Integration and Operations

Using the role criticality matrix below, determine how critical the person or role is to deal success.

Role Criticality Ratings

Rating	Impact on Integration (Short-Term)	Impact on Operations (Long-Term)
5 (Significant)	The integration will not occur if the position is vacant.	The business cannot meet its mission. The role is part of succession planning.
4 (Major)	The vacancy will result in significant cost increases or schedule slips.	The business will miss critical financial objectives. The role is likely on a succession plan.
3 (Moderate)	Some cost increases will occur, and integration may be slightly delayed as a result of the vacancy.	The vacancy will impact customers. The role requires a skilled incumbent.
2 (Minor)	Other employees will experience some pain, but the team will find ways to work around the vacancy.	
1 (Negligible)	Very few people would notice the vacancy.	

Prioritize Go-To-Market Strategy

SALES LEAD

The go-to-market strategy is probably the most important part of integration planning, which is why it is one of the first things to start planning. Think about why people acquire companies, it's usually because of a product, set of customers, or skills. Hence, planning should start with what that newly acquired set will look like post-close.

If you don't know what type of customers you are serving with the newly combined product, or you don't know what the combined product will look like, then you won't be able to decide which systems, people, skills, and processes are necessary to make everything work.

A go-to-market strategy should also involve cost structures which are key inputs to the valuation model. It is imperative that you have, even at a high level, a go-to-market (GTM) strategy before close.

Importance of GTM Strategy

"If you don't have a go-to-market strategy, you have no business closing the deal.

Some people fall into the trap of figuring it out after the fact. But I think you've got to at least have an idea in your head before you close:

How are you going to price this new product that you're acquiring?

Are you going to pursue a direct sales model or indirect sales model?

What are the cost structures associated with that?

All of that is a key part of the valuation model that corp dev's building, and they can make or break a deal.

It's okay to be in a position where you're not entirely sure of the nitty-gritty details, but you at least need to be able to identify what are the key things that we're going to have to figure out a bit of the post-close."

— Sabeeh Khan, Director, Corporate Strategy & Development at Syniti

---

Overlooking the GTM strategy and thinking you can figure it out post-close is a big mistake. This is also often due to the fact that most people believe that the deal thesis itself is the GTM strategy. The deal thesis is a broad overview of what you want to happen post-close. The GTM strategy is the step-by-step process of achieving the deal thesis. Make sure that you have an executable go-to-market strategy for day two.

Deal thesis vs. GTM Strategy

"A mistake that can be made is mistaking a thesis for a go-to-market strategy. The thesis is great as an initial conversation driver, but that go-to-market is skipping to the next level.

That's also a place where super clear ownership comes into play. Corporate Development can lead with a thesis and explain what's interesting, but the product team needs to be smarter and is able to put together the framework that drives everything else that the integration does post-close, and it should drive synergy planning.

Without that go-to-market, integration is toast. It takes forever to get through some of that stuff post-close. But it can be a relatively painless process if we do it pre-close."

— Aaron Whiting, M&A Integration and Strategic Programs at ContinuumCloud

---

So, how do you build a go-to-market strategy? It starts by getting your house in order and understanding how your organization brings products to market. When you acquire a product from another business, it will come with different standards from the way you operate.

Whether it's infrastructure, operating criteria, billing models, or legal terms, no two companies will have the same operating structure. Your job is to build a bridge to bring in that acquired product and make it successful in your organization.

The key is to communicate with the functions inside your organization and understand what it will take for them to fully integrate the incoming product. Those will be your function-specific integration plans that make up the go-to-market strategy.

How to Build your Go-to-Market Strategy

"It's really important that you understand how you bring things to market. The key is to take time and get inputs from folks internally who have that knowledge, who aren't M&A specific, to understand the common pieces that typically tie into an acquisition within your company.

These are the people focused on sales ops, focused on commercial legal, HR, etc.

I refer to this as the baseline deliverables. They are the common denominator and the things that you need to plan around for every specific function.

So, as you are supporting the project in-flight, the trick is to start capturing the baseline deliverables along the way. That will then help you build a spreadsheet of the things that your function requires to get to their integrated state, whatever the end state may be depending on the deal scenario and the go-to-market strategy."

— Gwen Pope, Head of Global Product M&A at eBay

Finalize Integration Budget

INTEGRATION LEAD

Documenting the integration budget should start earlier during diligence. This is a live document that should be continuously updated as you receive more information towards the end of the confirmatory due diligence process. The more information you have, the more accurate the integration budget can be.

Most companies estimate their integration costs based on previous deals or a percentage of the overall purchase price. This is the fastest and easiest way to come up with an integration budget and is also the most inaccurate one.

Common Mistakes in Integration Budgeting

"What a lot of corporate development or investment banking resources will do, is put in an estimate for integration costs that's either roughly what it was on the last deal or a percentage of the deal cost.

Neither one of those tends to be a good estimate of what it's actually going to take to do the integration, especially the percentage approach.

I can give an example. There were two deals that I did back in the 90s, that were both in the same billion-dollar price range.

One was two large food companies and the other one was a copper mine in Indonesia and a gold mine in Africa. Obviously, the food companies integrated completely, purchasing, distribution, and the more integration they did, the more synergies they realized.

But there was very little integration for the mining companies because it wasn't practical to do so. It was just a little bit of back-office integration.

So, even though the prices were very similar, the integration budget and timeline are very much different. This is why you can greatly benefit from having the integration personnel involved early."

— Kelly Haggerty, Founder of Nearco Transaction Advisors, LLC.

No two deals are the same. This means the level of integration will vary, depending on the deal rationale and the target company. Even if you have two very similar companies to integrate, there will always be differences between the businesses.

Different companies will have different quality of equipment, HR systems, and infrastructure, among other things. They will also have different locations, which will have many implications for the integration cost.

The best approach to budgeting integration is to map out the actual costs that you have, and will, incur which is known as the bottom-up approach. This would require reaching out to different functional areas and working with them to identify costs associated with their specific functions.

Play # 7 — Budgeting Integration

❖ **Description** - Find out how to effectively determine integration cost. Avoid and prepare for often overlooked costs and integrate the target company properly.

❖ **Author** - Galina Wolinetz

About the play

This play is designed to prepare for the costs of integration that many overlook.

Preparation

Aside from the strategic rationale that the business development team has developed as to why they would like to do a certain transaction, they need to make financial sense out of it.

Teams are often too focused on the synergies. They forget that there is a cost to achieving those synergies and integrating the target company properly.

Use this play to properly assess your potential integration cost. Execute this play towards the end of due diligence, after you have gathered enough information about the target company. The integration cost model should not be overlooked and is an intricate part of the business case.

You need to consider all the post-close integration issues, which you can break down into two categories: one-time costs and recurring costs.

People: Finance, Integration lead, deal sponsor, HR

Materials: Team collaboration, creativity, math skills

Difficulty: Medium

Time: 7 days

Running the Play

1. Brainstorming

    As you approach the end of due diligence and have gathered enough information about the complexity of the target company, it's time to plan your integration cost model. Work closely with HR, Finance, all other functions, and the deal sponsor to gather potential integration costs.

2. One Time Costs

    One of the very first costs that you should consider is the one-time costs. These are typically the costs necessary to fully integrate the target into your organization but will only take place once and are not intended to be ongoing costs post-close.

3. External support for the integration

4. Day one events

5. Upgrades to the target company to bring to your standards

6. Miscellaneous

7. Recurring Costs

   These are the ongoing additional costs that you will incur to maintain the acquired business.

8. IT

9. HR

10. Real Estate

11. Others, as appropriate

12. Finalizing

   As you come up with the projected integration cost model, compare it to your synergy model, so you can assess if the deal itself is still viable after incorporating all the costs.

Perform Premortems

DEAL LEAD

Another best practice that high-level professionals are doing is premortems. Executives too often celebrate too early post LOI. This is a good exercise to build that sense of urgency into the risks around the deal.

Premortem is an exercise where everyone assumes that the deal has already failed. Work your way backward to determine potential risks that can cause failure and what steps you can take to mitigate those risks.

Executing Premortems

"I have a premortem for every deal.

At the beginning of the deal, you do this together with the executives and you say, things went terribly south, what happened?

It's a really good thought exercise around the risks because a lot of people, especially at that time, are all excited. They're all happy getting term sheets and it's a lot of money, and how do we communicate this all? There's a lot of focus on the immediate.

So, create a mindset around thinking about how far you think into the future. We talked a lot about the success criteria for this deal. But let's flip the coin real quick and assume everything went terribly south.

And I really like premortems because they really shift the mindset and also help the team to come together and work better as a leadership team."

— Christian Von Bogdandy, Senior Director at Slalom

Section 3.7: Providing Governance

INTEGRATION
LEAD

The steering committee plays a huge role in ensuring integration success. On a finer point, it is the steering committee's job to navigate you, your workstream leads, and this initiative in the appropriate direction. Providing guidance and sage advice is one thing. This team will also need to step up in making key decisions.

Even though this group of advisors is activated after the deal is closed, getting their commitment and building the steering committee pre-close is highly recommended.

How to build a steering committee

Since this group oversees the success of the integration, getting the right people on this team is vital. Keep in mind that the people involved should be tailored to the specific needs of the transaction. The size of this team can also vary, depending on the deal. Here are some of the considerations to think about when choosing people, according to Tomer Stavitsky, Corporate Development, M&A Lead at Intuitive Surgical.

- Deal goals

- Timeline of the Deal

- The complexity of both companies

- Culture of the Target company

- Corporate Structure

- Issues found in diligence

- Integration tasks

The deal sponsor is typically the head of the steering committee because they will be responsible for the entire business on a go-forward basis.

A real-life example of how to build your steering committee:

"Let's say, for example, you are buying a company that is currently in a development stage. They don't have a product in the market, but we actually need them to develop something for us that is going to be integrated into our product. Think about this as a development effort, but also a commercialization effort.

In this case, I would treat them as a development company that doesn't have a lot of commercialization experience. They are also a startup, which means they want to move fast.

In this particular case, I am going to let them move very fast. I'm not going to handicap them with a very complex steering committee, and I'm going to keep a very close eye on the development.

I'm going to have a senior development person on that steering committee from my own company side, along with the head of R&D or the CTO of the other company because development is important here.

What's also important is commercialization. How does the development of that feature get integrated into the product? Therefore, I'm also going to have a commercial person who has a lot of experience in commercializing these sorts of products from my own company side on that steering committee. The focus of that steering committee is then going to be driving forward that development and thinking about the commercialization strategy. It's going to be composed mostly of people that handle the development and commercialization from both sides.

The goal of these commercial and development people from my side is to keep the other people accountable. They are going to be able to execute on time and we're going to be able to monitor their execution on time and step in to help along the way if there's any issues, if there's any concerns, if anybody is hitting a wall or something needs to be changed.

— *Tomer Stavitsky, Corporate Development, M&A Lead at Intuitive Surgical*

Below is a play that you can execute to help build the steering committee:

Play # 8 — Setting Up a Steering Committee

❖ **Description:** Learn how to set up bulletproof Guidance, Recommendations, and Leadership to assure successful outcomes from the acquisition. It is tailored for your specific integration.

❖ **Author:** John Morada, COO at M&A Science

About the play

It is time to demystify the purpose of a steering committee.

In many shapes and forms, a Steering Committee performs the duty of providing guidance, recommendations, and leadership to drive successful outcomes from the acquisition.

There are always groups within any acquirer who want an acquisition to be successful. The "group" can be two people or more.

A steering committee does not have to feel or look like a formal board. As a matter of fact, the less it has the formality of a Board, then the more fluid and flexible it can operate within Agile practices.

Setting up a steering committee ("SteerCo") will involve several steps of preparation. At the outset, there is the planning effort to establish an operating model tailored to your current Integration. Second, you will want to list nominees. Last but not least is the cadence of how often to convene.

Preparation:

Items listed in the materials section consist of easy logistical items to acquire. You will find that having this information ahead of time will provide efficiency gains when running the play.

For example, already having access to see calendar availability to key nominees will allow you to see which executives have the bandwidth to be part of the SteerCo.

People: Head of Integrations, Acquisition Executive Sponsor, Acquisition Market Sponsor, Corporate Development Lead

Difficulty: Complex

Materials: Buy plan, Team member list, DACI matrix template, SteerCo operating model template, access to see calendar availability.

Time: 3 hours

Running the Play:

1. Definite your Operating Model

   Governance structures should not be overly complicated.

   Often, integration teams do not want to set up a steerco for the fear of defining how the group would operate and what it would govern.

   Most small to mid-sized acquisitions do not require that much detail. Certainly, a good governance structure will be thorough and flexible.

   To the point of thoroughness, here are several must-have sections of your governance structure in no specific order:

Section	Why?
Team	Include in this document the team members of the SteerCo. You may find it useful to include why the individual's role is relevant to the Integration.
Confidentiality	Explain in good detail, ask Legal even, what can and cannot be made public from the SteerCo meetings. For example, do you want to publish all meeting notes? Which decisions need to be communicated downward versus upward?
Governance	An open-door policy is always good to raise concerns, risk and issues to a member of the SteerCo. But consider putting parameters around what immediate actions or decisions an individual is allowed to make without the consent of the SteerCo.
Communication	It is very important to define how the SteerCo will report upwards and govern downwards. Through proper communication protocols, the team members will know when to defer or own the messaging to respective parties. This mitigates any ambiguity. Also, the SteerCo will create a command presence that goes beyond any individual member.
Operating Model	Define in this section how the Committee will go about operating each meeting. Will you use Robert's Rules of Order? Will this be more Scrum-style stand-up?
Responsibilty	The normal definition of a SteerCo's role and responsibility must be included.

When it comes to an operating model, there is not a one-size-fits-all stamp. It is best to look at past SteerCo's to pull what you find will work well within your current Integration.

There are times when a five-page document works just as well for a $250 million acquisition as for a $5 billion acquisition. However, the content in each is tuned to the needs of the integration, the players, and the stakeholders.

2. Draft Your Nominees

Finding and getting an agreement with the SteerCo nominees may be the hardest part of this play for you. It is not difficult because of the complexity but rather the politics that could be involved when socializing the list.

Here is some advice on how best to avoid lengthy arguments about why you selected certain names:

- Create a transparent and safe environment for the conversation about the nominees. There is no sense in holding one-off chats to garner support since that just leads to back-channel distrust.

- Everyone needs to be open to feedback and, if needed, apply Chatham House Rules for confidentiality.

- Flush out where there are political motives and stop it.

- Seek out Executives who have the bandwidth. Do some research by accessing their available calendars or EAs ahead of time.

- Take note of the personality characteristics of each nominee.

- Determine which personalities can complement your goals for achieving a fast and agile method for this Integration.

- Write down the characteristics of successful Committee members, since this will be key to assessing whether nominees make the mark.

Expect your nominee list to go through at least one revision. If you did your homework well, then the changes will not be major. Have an open mind and listen. Maybe you will learn something new that makes a nominee better or worse from your initial assessment.

Involved in the confirmation effort of your nominations should be the acquisition executive sponsor, the acquisition market sponsor, and the corporate development lead.

3. Set the Cadence on SteerCo Meetings

Armed with the confirmed list of SteerCo members, you can begin the effort to plan the recurring meetings. This is a simple effort to look through calendars to find what day and time works for everyone.

Please make sure to find a time when you cannot question mandatory SteerCo attendance. It is very important to have the highest attendance possible.

In terms of timing, the decision to make it weekly or monthly can be challenging. More flexibility in this selection seems to work for most.

At the outset, hold SteerCo meetings every other week for two months. This gives you and the SteerCo plenty of time to cement how to operate as a team while keeping the frequency of conversations, topics, and decisions moving forward in the early days. Then around the three-month mark, switch the SteerCo cadence to monthly.

Section 3.8: Day one preparations

INTEGRATION
LEAD

Day one is, in many cases, the first time for non-deal participants to know details about the acquisition. Have a good communication plan to avoid panic from every party affected by the transaction. This would include your own employees, the acquired workforce, and the incoming customers and vendors. The key is to make a good impression since the goal is to retain both employees and customers and keep the business running like business-as-usual.

Communication Plan

The communication team should ideally be in charge of the overall communication plan. If you don't have a communication team, assign this to the HR and marketing departments. The HR department will be in charge of internal communications since they are more in touch with the employees. The external team is better linked to the marketing department, which are more customer-facing.

If you are a publicly held company, do not announce the deal internally much before the external announcement. You can get in trouble for insider trading. The internal and external announcements should all happen simultaneously in one day.

How this messaging goes will play a huge role in retaining employees, which is one of the biggest value drivers of the deal. To truly capture the value of the acquired business, you need to be able to retain the

COMMUNICATIONS LEAD people that made the company great.

It's no secret that people inherently don't like change, especially if you are forcing the change upon them. In their minds, you are the villain in the story and just rocked their world. This is the common narrative that you need to change on this monumental day.

Common reactions from employees are fear, uncertainty, and doubt. Your job is to mitigate those feelings using well-crafted messaging. Failing to do so will result in people leaving, and you will end up spending more money and time replacing people who will leave.

Work with the communication team and craft a good message to be delivered on day one. Here are best practices that you can use for effective communication:

Consistent Messaging

Some leaders who are very good and comfortable at speaking publicly can do an impromptu speech. However, this exposes you to inconsistent messaging and potential errors and will result in a loss of trust from the acquired employees.

Well-Crafted Messaging

"If you're able to communicate the why? What is it going to look like? How are we going to get there? And most importantly, what are the people's parts in it? If you have a clear vision of the future and a credible plan to get there, people will tend to follow you."

— **David Olsson, Partner at Beyond the Deal**

Do not wing the announcement day messaging. Use prepared talking points, so that everybody on your side has the same message and answers to every question thrown your way. Talk about what matters to the employees. We've seen leaders focus on the deal rationale of the transaction, which employees don't care about, for the entire duration of their speech. At some point, employees from both companies will wonder, "What happens to me?" Empathy and willingness to answer these questions ahead of them being asked will assuage some concerns but not all. Consider doing smaller-group meetings, where the intimate setting creates a safe harbor for employees to voice their thoughts and feelings.

Empathy

The most common mistake that leaders make is coming in with a certain amount of hubris during announcement day. It comes across that you are better than them because you just acquired them.

The reality is that you need the employees to stay. You can only do that if you show empathy in your messaging.

It is crucial to put yourself in the shoes of the employees. Not everyone got a big fat paycheck for selling the company. There will always be people who have a negative outlook on the deal. Manage these people rather than antagonize them, which could escalate the situation.

The Power of Saying I don't know

"You want to start building trust with those employees that have concerns. If you have someone who's particularly outspoken in a negative way asking questions at a town hall or a training event, answer their questions. If you don't know the answer to the question, let that person know that you don't know and that you'll find an answer and get it to them. You want to be the person who understands what's difficult about this transition and helps make it as less painful as it can possibly be."

— Briana Elkington, Sr. Manager, M&A Integration Management Office at Community Psychiatry

---

The Power of a Middle Manager

It is no surprise that the employees do not trust the acquirer. The importance of having a trusted messenger in the incoming company is something that people often overlook. High executive leaders, especially the owner, who got compensated for selling the company, are not going to be credible messengers. You need to unlock the power of middle managers.

Importance of Middle Manager

"Middle managers are really the secret to successful integration."

— Klint Kendrick, HR M&A Leader with several Fortune 500 firms

---

Middle managers are the most trusted source of information for employees. Since they are the ones in the trenches with people, they are the best people to advocate for the upcoming changes.

The power of Middle Managers

"No one's going to listen to anyone from the company that's acquiring, as much as someone within their own company."

— Briana Elkington, Sr. Manager, Growth Integration & Diligence Team at Mindpath Health

---

Two to three weeks before the announcement, talk to the middle managers and prepare them for the inevitable transition. Once you get the middle managers to trust the acquisition, they will be the ones to settle the employees' nerves on announcement day.

If you want to have a seamless announcement day, execute the play below and be fully prepared for this very crucial day.

Play # 9: Setting Up Employee Announcement

❖ **Description:** This play is designed to fully prepare your company to announce the deal to employees.

❖ **Play By:** Klint Kendrick

About the play

Retaining acquired employees is one of the most crucial elements of driving value in most deals. An unhappy workforce is not a productive —or profitable—workforce, which causes value leaks in your acquisition.

This is why the employee announcement is absolutely critical. People, by nature, don't like change. The moment you announce the deal, people will start to feel panic, stress, and fear.

Run this play to help employees prepare for the changes that will come after announcement day. Prepare to face employees' tough questions and gain their trust. Strategically schedule your announcement and prepare middle management to assist with the transition.

Preparation

People: Integration Lead, Deal Sponsor, Acquired Middle Managers, HR, CEO

Difficulty: Difficult

Materials: Team collaboration, Creativity, Pen, and Paper.

Time: 2 weeks (when possible)

Running the play:

1. Prepare your messaging

   Do not wing your announcement day messaging. You need to have prepared FAQs and talking points to avoid misinformation and to cover all bases that need to be covered.

   Many leaders begin by taking a victory lap, discussing how the acquisition furthers the company strategy. While these can be important things to communicate, realize that employees are usually in a state of shock, and they are unlikely to be receptive to long business discussions.

   Instead, move quickly to the three major concerns of the employees:

2. Do I still have a job?

3. Will the acquiring management team be fair to me?

4. Will my job be as good – especially in terms of compensation, benefits, work environment, and company culture?

   The FAQ document should go into detail about changes the employees will experience. If you don't know the answer to a question, they are likely to ask, don't make it up. Be honest and let employees know you are working out the details.

   As you prepare the materials, take a moment and imagine yourself in the acquired employee's shoes. How would you want to be treated? What questions would you need to be answered?

5. Prepare middle managers

   Middle managers are the best-kept secret of successful integrators. Before the employee announcement, prepare the middle managers of the target company and start their own change process by answering the three major questions for them.

   You should also give the middle managers a sense of what their team members are about to go through and give them tools and support to lead their team through the change. This can include mini-change management training and a preview of the FAQs.

   Remember, you're relying on the middle managers to be your trusted messengers. They will help to settle the freaked-out employees on announcement day.

6. Prepare swag

Giving out swag helps employees emotionally assimilate. Prepare T-shirts, mouse pads, coffee mugs, or anything that will help them align with their new identity as a member of the acquiring company.

7. Prepare schedule

You need to strategically schedule your announcement. Wait too long, and the rumor mill will start to catch up. Employees learning about the deal from somewhere else is not a good start for your acquisition.

8. Deliver the message

Take all of the prep work you've done and execute with empathy.

External Announcement

COMMUNICATIONS LEAD

External communication is where you will be announcing to the world that you just bought the target company, typically in a press release. Aside from this, you should also be sending emails to the acquired customers for a more personal touch.

When reaching out to clients, it is important to address their most important concern, how does this transaction impact them and their day-to-today operations? Educate them about the deal rationale, so they have an understanding of the changes and some of the things that they can look forward to in the future.

Here is a sample template that you can use,

Sample Client Notification

Dear [client]:

We are pleased to announce our forthcoming [merger or acquisition] with _____. It is scheduled to take place officially on [insert date].

[Insert paragraph of information about the history of your organization.]

[Insert 2 sentences about why you have decided to merge or acquire.]

[Insert 2 sentences about the synergies the two firms will be tapping into.]

[Insert information about any changes to services] We will be able to provide you with many new services and areas of expertise in the future. We look forward to discussing those in more depth with you.

However, there are several things we want to point out that will not change:

- You will continue to work with the same people in our organization you have in the past. We retain all of our people in their current roles.

- Your fees and costs associated with our organization will not change.

- The services we have provided you in the past will continue to be offered by the new organization. [Insert information about new location, website, logo, etc.]

We are thrilled to continue doing business with you and appreciate your continued partnership.

Regards,
[CEO signature]

Internal Communication

Arguably the most crucial part of the announcement is communicating the acquisition with the employees on both sides. Create a strong yet empathetic message for the CEO to deliver on day one.

Focus less on corporate strategies and synergies because the message is for the employees who are emotionally invested in the company. Focus more on the changes that will happen, and make sure that all the information is consistent and accurate. The last thing you want is to deliver a wrong message and break trust during this process.

COMMUNICATIONS LEAD

Do not neglect the employees. Most of them might also be afraid of the acquisition, as new incoming employees might take their place in the organization. The goal is to put them at ease during announcement day.

Here is a sample welcome letter that you can use,

Sample Welcome Letter

Dear [Company name] employees:

I'd like to welcome you to (Name of the new company). We are excited to journey on this venture with you as we start the business as a new entity. I trust that this letter finds you mutually excited about your new employment with (Name of Company).

I'd also like to welcome you to the [name of new company] on behalf of all of the staff at [other company]. Each of us will play a role to ensure the successful integration of [other company] with our current operations.

The next few months will be challenging and exciting, as we work together towards new goals. Please reach out to your manager or human resources for any concerns or ideas on how we can improve the overall state of our new organization.

As we develop new company policies, benefits, and ideas around our specific culture, we are committed to communicating with you about them every step of the way. You should begin to receive communications around these topics shortly.

Again, welcome to the team. We look forward to having you come on board.

Regards,
[CEO signature]

Section 3.9: Closing

DEAL LEAD

Signing and immediately closing rarely happen in a transaction. There are usually conditions that are needed to be satisfied before you can close the deal (A.K.A. — conditions precedent to closing). The most common ones are regulatory approval and getting consent for contract transfers, such as rent or vendor contracts.

Regulatory approvals are commonly known as antitrust risk. It is a government committee that is responsible for making sure that businesses are competing fairly. In short, if you are a threat to monopolizing your industry through the current acquisition, they will veto the deal entirely. While you are waiting for this consent, there is pretty much nothing you can do to speed it up.

The legal team is the one responsible for the completion of these closing conditions. However, be aware that the longer it takes to close, the more risk you are wearing. You are currently in a gray area where the business is bound to be yours, everybody already knows about the transaction, but it's not completed.

In this situation, you have no recourse in case of any material degradation of the business. No matter how much you try to put covenants around how they are going to operate the business, there will be attrition.

The best thing to do is try and close the deal as fast as possible. The following is a play that you can execute for a faster and smoother closing:

Play # 10 — Signing and Closing

❖ **Description:** Learn about organizing the process, obtaining signatures, and drafting and negotiating all closing documents. Bring attention to detail and preparation.

❖ **Author:** Toby Tester

About the play

A smooth signing and closing require careful detail and preparation. Organize the exercise well, so that last-minute issues do not hold up the process.

The signing and closing process is typically the responsibility of the legal function. They take on the responsibility for organizing the process, obtaining signatures, and drafting and negotiating all closing documents.

Preparation:

The legal function typically compiles a deal completion checklist from the sharer and purchase agreement. This document summarizes all the activities that one must complete before closing. The steps outlined here are typical as part of the closing process.

People: Executive sponsor, separation manager, and deal team

Difficulty: Medium

Materials: Meeting Agenda, Whiteboard, Strategy Documents

Time: Spend one day or more preparing materials for a two-hour play.

Running the Play:

1. Obtain Necessary Consents

    All required regulatory approvals and third-party consents, such as transfers of contracts, that have a change of control provision and, therefore, require consent will need to be secured. Private transactions typically do not require regulatory approval.

2. Confirm Representations and Warranties

    The other party's representations and warranties will have been true when made and remain true at closing, and they will require that the other party will have complied with its pre-closing covenants.

3. Obtain Board and Shareholder Approvals

    Board or shareholder approvals are required in most transactions to affect the transaction, in addition to any contractual or statutory requirements that you have to meet. If opinions of counsel are to be supplied by each party to the other party, the law firms supplying the opinions need to complete due diligence.

4. Obtain Certificates and Filings as Appropriate

Obtain certificates regarding the validity of the corporations entering into the agreements. Make filings with the applicable government and regulatory entities in the appropriate jurisdictions. This will satisfy any laws in those jurisdictions.

5. Ensure Transaction Documents are Executed

6. Confirm Payment Consideration is Available

Section 3.10: Post-mortem Reviews

In the interest of continuous improvement, post-mortem reviews are crucial in finding out what went wrong in a deal and why it turned out the way it did. Without an opportunity to examine what happened, your team will follow the same process and will commit the same mistake again.

Since post-mortems come after a problem, it's going to be a lot easier to accomplish and get buy-in from people who will be involved in the process. The goal is to identify and learn from the problem for future use and not to place blame on anyone.

This review is often a mode of reporting for leaders who may or may not be involved in the transaction itself.

Retrospectives

In Agile M&A, you don't have to wait for something to go wrong before you review past performances. Reflect on your past or even ongoing deals. These are called retrospectives.

Retrospectives are a great tool to look back at what happened and improve even when the deal goes smoothly. Don't wait for the deal to finish. Some companies do retrospectives in the middle of deals, some do it weeks after the deal is closed, and other companies, like Harris, do it a year after the deal is closed. Over at Harris, they call these meetings a post-acquisition review.

Importance of a Post-Acquisition Review

"The best process we have that was created by Constellation a few years ago, is called PAR. Post-Acquisition Review.

We typically do this about a year after we've completed the acquisition and we've operated the business and we sit down, and we just go back through all of our major assumptions that we made during diligence.

What did we learn? Did we make a good assumption? If we did, what did we learn from it? Did we make a bad assumption? Why, at the time, were we comfortable making that assumption, or what did we do to validate it? Then we try to share those learnings with everyone else."

— Jeff Bender, CEO at Harris.

This is typically only for people involved in the transaction and is not a formal report required by upper management. However, this is one of the best ways you can improve your team, process, and retain best practices.

Importance of Retrospectives

"In every deal that we do, we will do a retrospective. I am the first one to say, even though I have done this for over 20 years, that I am not perfect. I know that there are great lessons learned on every deal and things that we could do better. I think that is important."

— Jeremy Segal, Senior Vice President of Corporate Development at Progress

---

Here's how to do retrospectives:

Play # 11 — Retrospective

❖ **Description** — Gauge the effectiveness of deal processes and tools to determine a plan for future improvement.

❖ **Author** — Kison Patel, CEO and founder of M&A Science

About the Play

Truly developing and maintaining a culture of continuous improvement and refinement is difficult to achieve, yet vital for M&A functions to deliver reliable maximum value.

Implementing retrospectives, a fundamental Agile practice, can enable practitioners to extract important lessons from M&A deals and proactively enforce them to improve future outcomes.

Retrospectives are meetings that take place during deal milestones or after the deal closes to review what is working well and what is not, as well as to consider how to improve on the process.

The goal of retrospectives is to gauge the effectiveness of deal processes and tools and to determine a plan for future improvement. These open discussions help to identify ways to improve processes and strengthen team alignment.

Team members' morale increases when they feel like others are hearing them, and they will likely have substantive follow-through on ideas they generate themselves.

Preparation

People: All members of a team/workstream

Difficulty: Easy to moderate

Materials: Homework, whiteboard/large paper

Time: Approximately an hour and a half (including prep time)

Running the Play

1. Do your homework

    30 minutes pre-meeting:

    To put the retrospective into play, set time aside to meet with your team (all team members from a single team should be present, and the meeting should come at the end of an iteration or a predefined project milestone/checkpoint), and send the questions you will ask ahead of time, so that team members can reflect and prepare their responses.

    Questions should include:

    - "What worked really well for this deal?"
    - "What lessons have we learned that we can apply to the next deal?"
    - "What did not work this time that we should avoid doing on the next deal?"

2. Open the Meeting with an Emphasis on Openness

    5 minutes: Beginning the meeting with an emphasis on openness and positivity is key. There has to be a desire to be better and to listen to all team members, not just senior members, and not focus solely on positives and/or negatives.

3. Focus on Workflow and Team Dynamics

20 minutes: Focus conversation on issues that affect workflow and team dynamics.

4. Analyze Effectiveness

   15 minutes: Analyze the effectiveness of any plays fielded and brainstorm potential adjustments.

5. Look Closely at the North Star Strategic Goals

   15 minutes: Discuss how successful the team has been in aligning lower-level work with the overarching strategic goal of the initiative.

6. Additional Items

   10 minutes: Review any other pertinent items affecting the team's effectiveness and processes.

7. Incorporate Lessons Learned

   The timing of this step will vary based on how the retrospective is applied and who is responsible for follow-up.

A big part of what makes a successful M&A function is to have the ability to execute numerous deals successfully. You don't want to keep repeating the same mistakes from past deals.

That's also not to say that there will always be deals on the table for you and your company. There will be times when the target refuses to sell, or there isn't just anything out there for your strategic needs.

At this point, your corporate development team is pretty much-doing nothing. The worst thing that can happen and what you want to avoid is people losing their M&A knowledge. Having these sprint meetings and reviewing past deals is highly beneficial.

Another problem that most organizations face is retaining tribal knowledge. When people leave an organization, the knowledge and experience go with them. Knowledge retention and being able to share information across all functions are crucial for your M&A team. Although other companies might have different names, for the purposes of this book, we will call it an M&A center of excellence. If you want to learn more about it, go to page 165.

Chapter 4

Culture

Deals should never end without taking a pass at culture. This is something that gets thrown out a lot in the world of M&A but often gets overlooked. When you hear of failed deals, it's usually because of culture. What does it really mean, and how does it affect deals?

In its simplest form, culture is how things get done. Culture encompasses everything including values, work habits, communications, decision-making, processes, and behaviors. When you buy a company, you're not just buying the P&L of the company, you're also buying the culture. You're buying their product, go-to-market strategy, and more often than not, you are buying their management team. This is why cultural fit is crucial in any deal.

However, there are still a lot of practitioners who don't believe in culture. They believe that culture is overrated and used as a scapegoat for failed deals. The fact of the matter is, if you combine two companies and ignore contrasting cultures, it could lead to value destruction. There are major risks when it comes to culture, operational risk, and people risk.

Section 4.1: Operational Risk

The first thing to look at is the operational risk. This is where you assess how changes in the way you do work are going to impact the combined company's ability to deliver products and services to customers.

How Culture Risk affects Deal Value

"We purchased a company, at one of my prior employers, that built drones. Their procurement process was, that they would go down to Napa auto parts and they would buy the pieces that they needed to build these prototype drones.

But after you pull them into a larger organization, that's a government contractor that has very specific rules about how you buy things, then all of a sudden, a process that used to take two hours, now takes weeks.

Now you have to get supplier approval. You have to make sure that the part is in the catalog. These are important elements of culture that often get overlooked. And then when you get into operating the post-integration business, all of a sudden, you're wondering why you're not delivering things on time."

— Klint Kendrick, HR M&A Leader with several Fortune 500 firms

Klint's story is a perfect example of the reason why big companies almost always unintentionally destroy small companies during an acquisition. The overlaying of bureaucracies and approval processes to the smaller companies can be detrimental to how they work and what makes them successful.

Common Challenges to Cultural Integration

"The most common issues, when big companies acquire small ones, are the layering in of the bureaucracies, the decision-making and the approval processes that take much longer.

There are reasons why those processes are put in place for larger companies, but for a smaller one, it doesn't necessarily make sense.

Like applying an allocation of shared services overhead to an acquired business. You've got a large IT organization, which certainly wouldn't be justified for such a small company, which maybe had one or two people managing most of their IT and outsourcing a lot. Now they have an allocation charge that they didn't have.

That's just another example of the kinds of inefficiencies perhaps that you can introduce inadvertently."

— Jeff Desroches, Vice President, Strategy & Corporate Development at VAT GROUP

Operational risks, just like any other risks, tend to get more complicated when you are doing an international deal. Aside from differences in management approach, international laws vary from country to country and could play a huge role in integrating businesses.

Biggest Red Flag on International Deals

"The biggest thing I always worry about, when doing international deals, is the foreign corrupt practices act (FCPA).

You always have to make sure that companies aren't giving kickbacks to government employees. They're not taking bribes and things of that nature. And you have to be able to find a good accounting firm or you can even look for it yourself, to go through the P&L, the balance sheet, et cetera, to look for little hints of things that could occur.

Because that is a definite no-no for US companies to even buy a company that violated FCPA. You can get fined for just buying the company. And it happens, international people do business differently, bribes and kickbacks are part of the culture."

— Jeff Baker, Chief Financial Officer at Paysign, Inc.

This doesn't mean that big companies can't buy small companies successfully, or cultural differences will make deals impossible. It simply means you can't ignore these underlying problems, or you will end up destroying the very company you bought.

Reverse Diligence

One of the best practices that has been trending is the idea of reverse diligence. It simply means allowing the target company to get to know the parent company better. Tell them who you are, what you do, and how you are thinking about integrating their business.

This is crucial, especially for founder-owned businesses, because they love their company, and they would want to see it succeed. Hence, they will do everything in their power to help you grow the business. If you don't arm them with that information, then you're not setting them up to help you.

But most importantly, the best thing that you can do is to be transparent about non-negotiables. What are your "must-haves" — things that are absolutely necessary for you to be able to make the best out of the acquisition?

Subsequently, listen to the acquired company and what their non-negotiables are, the items that are necessary for them to be the same attractive company you bought in the first place.

Negotiating the Non-Negotiables

"It's really important that those non-negotiables are very clear.

The acquirer needs to help the acquired company understand what are the assets or products that they really need to preserve, things that are part of the deal rationale.

> *Make sure that everybody knows that you are not going to impose your operating model on these three or four things because those are the things that you really want to preserve.*
>
> *For the acquired company, it is also important to know what are the things that they shouldn't waste their time fighting. Because there will always be some form of integration.*
>
> *You don't want to end up acquiring companies and having 10 different processes for the same objectives."*
>
> **— Valeria Strappa, Regional Head of Liquidity and Account Solutions for the Americas | Managing Director at JPMorgan Chase & Co.**

Now, after laying down the non-negotiables and assessing the culture fit, you will get a better understanding of how you will work together post-close. In some instances, working together would seem impossible, and this will give you a chance to pull out of the deal sooner rather than later.

Section 4.2: People Risk

Losing employees post-close is the single, most impactful value leak in a deal. They are the ones that operate the business that you bought, so it is only logical that you need them post-close. In order to increase employee retention, you need to do a lot more than golden handcuffs.

Employee Retention

"We've got to keep people motivated, engaged and happy. Money alone isn't enough to keep people around. We gotta do a lot more than that."

— Christina Ungaro, Head of Corporate Development at JLL

This is where the HR manager needs to collaborate with the counterpart HR on the target company and start meeting the people inside the organization. What are the incentives that really matter? What career advancement opportunities are available? Identify what makes the employees happy inside the organization and what you can do for them to keep them happy. After all, a happy workforce will translate to more productivity.

Creating a Great Culture

"Culture and leadership development is the most significant piece of creating a competitive advantage. When your culture is great, more people stay over the long term, and you will end up getting more momentum in the business."

— Jason Lippert, CEO of LCI Industries.

This is why creating a great culture for employees to work in is crucial in every deal, and it begins with trust. If you can make employees feel comfortable about the changes and preserve what matters to them, then they will feel like they are really part of the new organization.

The Story about the Red Couch

"The conversations we have and the trust that you're building with the leaders and the employees as you go is critical. You have to do what you say you're going to do. If we say that we support their culture, then we should allow them to continue certain things.

We worked with a company with small teams in different locations. We had a small team located in one location that was moving into Microsoft office. They had their office in this home, they had all these cool personal things, and they had this red couch that when I went and visited their office and met with them, they told me the history and why they love this couch and what it means to them.

So, in my mind, if we tell them that we support and want them to be successful and we support their culture, I have to figure out how to bring that red couch.

It's a very small example, but if we tell people that they can be who they are, and then we limit that type of stuff, that can erode trust. So, we're constantly looking at how we back what we say, and that we want to learn from them and help them see what they can bring to Microsoft.

Kim Jones, Sr. HR M&A Manager at Microsoft

In order to mitigate all cultural risks, conduct an early assessment of whether or not the culture of the target company can fit into your organization or not. Execute this play to get an overview of the target company's culture.

Play # 12 — Cultural Assessment

❖ **Description:** This play is designed to give a quick overview of a target company's culture.

❖ **Play By:** Kison Patel

About the play

Cultures play a big factor when it comes to integration. In some cases, if the two cultures are not a fit, it can be a deal killer. Understand the similarities and differences between the two companies as early as possible.

Use this play to instantly have a high-level view of the target's culture, such as important integration criteria and factors to anticipate that can potentially impact the deal. This includes writing recommendations and assigning team members the items that you want to change for better integration.

Preparation

People: HR, Integration Leader, Corp dev

Difficulty: Difficult

Materials: Pen, paper, collaboration, survey sheets

Time: 2 weeks

Running the play:

1. Onsite observations

   As soon as the diligence starts, begin onsite observations. Roam around their offices, talk to the people, observe their processes, and make sure to take notes on anything that you can observe.

2. Conduct Surveys

   Conduct extensive surveys with specific questions to the entire company. Try to receive at least 90% participation in the surveys for more accuracy.

3. Focus group session

   Conduct a session with the people who are working on the integration and ask them your questions. This is a good way to make sure you have a variety of different people at the table.

4. One-on-one interview

   Work with HR or the leadership team to identify key people in different roles. This includes mid-level managers and frontline employees. Conduct one-on-one interviews for higher-quality information.

5. Write your report

   This is a template of what you need to be doing in your cultural assessment.

   Title

   Description

   Page 1 — Executive Summary Section

   Overview of the entire report. The purpose, objectives, and approach of cultural diligence.

   Page 2 — Similarity and difference section

   List down all the similarities and differences between the two cultures. (decision-making style, work environment, financial accountability, customer service approach, etc.)

   Page 3 — Cultural theme section

   Highlight key items about the culture that emerged from the data collection. (How they work together, relationships with co-workers, etc.)

   Page 4 — Paradox section

   Cultural behaviors that seem to contradict one another.

   Page 5 — Observation section

   Jot down their excitement and fears about joining your company.

   Page 6 — Recommendation section

A prioritized list of actions to help ensure cultural alignment.

6. Leadership Buy-in

   Make sure that you can get buy-in from the leadership team on your recommendations. Help them understand why it is important to have cultural alignment and how it will benefit both sides of the deal.

7. Implementation

   Inside your recommendation section, there should be a list of specific actions that your team is going to do to get that alignment. Assign a person that would be the owner of this workstream and set appropriate timelines.

8. Track the progress

   Track the progress of the implementation based on the timelines and a list of actionable items that you have set.

Chapter 5

M&A Center of Excellence

We dedicate this chapter to the head of corporate development, who is seeking to solidify their function and continuously improve the M&A process. If you want to continuously run deals efficiently, you need to learn from your past deals, whether they be mistakes or successful feats. Managing knowledge and past experiences are a great way to improve your process for future deals, and the best way to do this is to build an M&A center of excellence.

Section 5.1 — M&A Center of Excellence

If you want to take retrospectives to the next level and document everything, build an M&A center of excellence.

An M&A center is a repository of knowledge for your M&A practice. It could be a website, software program, or even a book. In its simplest form, an M&A center is where you keep M&A knowledge, best practices, past deal experiences, and anything regarding your M&A activities for future reference.

If you are a company that has an active portfolio and you have a commonality in your deals and strategy, having a center can be extremely beneficial. The idea is to document everything and put them in one place for everyone to contribute or gather information.

Just keep in mind, that it takes a lot of work and a lot of resources. Therefore, you need to have dedicated M&A experts to build and maintain the center.

Section 5.2 — Benefits of an M&A Center of Excellence

The primary benefit of having an M&A center of excellence is it allows you to capture best practices and lessons learned from all your deals and apply them effectively on the next transaction. Not only can you continuously improve your practice, but you also capture value better and faster.

Advantages of Building an M&A Center

"For us, we were looking to contribute to M&A success. We wanted to help improve the return on investment on our deals. And having a center provides us the opportunity to execute a cheaper, faster, and more effective integration.

We like to focus less on integration and spend more time on synergies. Having the knowledge repository and the center in place provides that foundation for us. It allows us to avoid mistakes, especially the repeated ones that are most frustrating. It allows us to capture and leverage past experiences and learnings to improve future execution.

So, for us, it's really all around capturing that knowledge, making sure we apply it so that we can improve our execution."

— Philip Pratt, Director, Acquisition Integration at Corning Incorporated

---

In addition to best practices, you can also use the M&A center as a point of reference for failed or difficult deals. You can look at past deals with risks that you were not able to mitigate or difficulties that you were not able to overcome. Having a point of reference can set expectations for current or future deals.

Advantages of Building an M&A Center

"When it comes to knowledge management, we have grown an M&A hub, as we call it. It started as we had data every year and it's everyone's problem. Data was everywhere. And the unfortunate thing is if someone left, the data went with them.

So, what we built is a multi-year plan. It's honestly taken us about four years to get to a place where data is all in one place. And we would like to get to a state where we can be more predictive around the risks that we may incur on future acquisitions based on our past performance. So, when you get to those very early meetings with the business teams, you are better educated.

And in the past, it would be the person that did that acquisition who has that knowledge. And they were the only ones that had that knowledge for the next acquisition. But not everyone has access to it. So now we get the power of the team."

— Karen Ashley, Vice President, Corporate Development Integration at Cisco.

Section 5.3 — Building an M&A Center of Excellence

An M&A center may vary from one organization to another. However, the basics of building one would pretty much be the same. Here's a high-level overview of how to build an M&A center of excellence, according to Philip Pratt, Director, Acquisition Integration at Corning Incorporated.

Develop the Initial Concept

The first step is to clearly define your concept of an M&A center. Is it a library? Is it an office? Is it a computer program? Whatever it is, formulate and finalize the vision before communicating it to anyone else.

Define the mission of the center. This will dictate which people should be involved and the tools needed to maintain the center. You also need to define the governance of the center. How will information go inside the center? How will you update and maintain the system? These are just some of the crucial decisions to make before involving other people.

Getting Buy-in

As previously mentioned, it takes a lot of work and people to build and maintain an M&A center of excellence. You can't do it alone. Educate people on the importance of the center and how it can make the M&A practice better and faster. With effective communication, you can generate excitement and gain the support of the people you need.

You need to get buy-in from the stakeholders and everyone that needs to be involved in the center itself. Recruit people that will happily devote their time to the center and assign roles and responsibilities.

Repository Box

After structuring the center and getting people on board, it's time to develop and formalize the repository box. This is where you are going to put all the M&A data for keeping and distribution.

No matter what it is, make sure that it is easy to use and intuitive because the information will be massive, especially in the long run, so users will need to find any information they need easily.

Maintaining the repository box is just as important as putting in new information. Continuously update the collateral, database, and files with best practices and new lessons learned throughout its lifetime. Some tools need to be updated more frequently than others and assigned team members need to be accountable for maintaining and updating the information in the center.

Maintenance can be an arduous task. Plenty of analysts perform this role or even interns. This can be a really good entry point for a junior yet top performer from the business line.

Launching

After the contents are all developed, and the database is ready to go, it is time to launch the center. Let the entire organization know that the center is up and running. Educate them about the benefits of the center and how it can help them in their practice. If people don't know about the center and why they should use it, no one will. Consider adding a short welcome video to the CoE site, if you decide to make it a website. Having a welcome message strongly conveys that you've thought about visitor needs. The welcome message should include:

- A genuine greeting
- What they can expect from the site
- Highlights of areas to visit first
- What they can expect going forward, e.g., subscribe to the site for news or find new reference material quarterly

A launch also needs to be socialized internally. Just like you use social media to share memories, put together a communications plan on how you want the recognition of the new CoE on all the internal comms channels. Then make friends with the admin for internal comms. That way, they can come back to you when they need new content for their newsletter, and you're top of mind.

Training

Finally, train people on how to use the database. Teach people how to add and find information, what are the contents of the center, and who are the people they can approach if they need any help. The only way people will utilize the center is if it's easy to use.

Chapter 6

Divestitures

No matter how hard you work or plan, there will always be unforeseen circumstances. It's safe to say that not every acquisition is going to be great. If, for whatever reason, you have gone after a bad acquisition, or due to unforeseen circumstances, a business in your organization is not performing at its best, you can always consider a divestiture.

Divestitures, a.k.a corporate carve-out, are a huge part of corporate development, especially if you are looking to transform the business. Strategies shift all the time, and divestitures are a highly profitable way of selling assets that are no longer part of your core strategy, and you can't maximize their full potential anymore. This way, you can raise capital and use it for other areas of your organization.

In the interest of maximizing the potential value of the business, it is important to note that you should avoid selling a business under duress. Not only will the business have low marketability and value, but it will also compel you to sell quickly without proper analysis and preparation. This is the mistake that most companies make.

Most companies have a notion that selling a business is a sign of failure, which causes them to be reluctant in divesting, especially if the business is still profitable. However, the reality is, that's the best time to sell the business.

Reluctance to Divestiture

"In a corporation, there's an inevitable pushback against the idea of selling, because selling is an admission of failure. And one of the things that we've seen over and over again is companies wait far too long to make the decision to sell because no one wants to admit there's a problem until the problem is pretty horrendous.

One of the best practices that we've seen is being really conscious and unbiased about evaluating your portfolio of businesses and identifying ones that could be for sale.

Also, try to separate the choice to sell a business from internal blame. Because if whoever has the business that's going to be sold is blameworthy, no one's going to want to have a saleable business.

So instead of just making the choice that something's not strategic, not a great fit anymore, it's not gonna grow, it even has a better home with somebody else, people tend to hang onto businesses too long.

Then when they decide to sell it's a fire sale. They can't do all the things to make the business more valuable and to make the sale more successful.

So inherent in a long preparation cycle is the self-awareness to think about what might be things that we want to divest. And how should we think about that potential for divestiture? It should be one of your strategic alternatives in any business that you have."

— Michael Frankel, SVP and Managing Director, Deloitte New-venture Accelerator / Deloitte Investments

Section 6.1 — Analysis

Being self-aware is one of the key elements in growing a business. Not only should you know exactly what your organization needs to grow, but you should also know the businesses that are no longer efficient.

These are the businesses that will no longer grow inside your company, and you should divest in the near future. Companies should be regularly evaluating whether any of their businesses could be divestiture candidates.

Importance of Annual Divestiture Analysis

"Companies have a duty to the shareholders, employees, and customers of a business that may not have a future under their ownership, to at least consider whether divestiture would help extract greater value for them and result in a better owner for that business.

Another reason to engage in a regular divestiture analysis is that successful divestitures require rigorous planning that could take many months.

And to accommodate all that plan, you need to identify the businesses that you may want to sell far in advance of when you may kick off an actual formal sale process. So, you should absolutely avoid rushing into a sale process.

You should avoid waiting to sell a business after the wheels have come off and it's traumatically underperforming, because in both of those cases, if you're rushed to sell a business, it's going to significantly reduce the value of that business. It's going to limit your potential buyer pool. They're going to be less people interested in a lower-value business. And so, you may be left with a group of interested buyers that you may not want.

So how regularly do you evaluate whether to divest? Annually seems like a good cadence. You can wrap it up with your normal annual strategic planning and budgeting processes. You've got a fresh set of financials and other operational metrics that you can look at at the end of the year, going into the following year."

— *Russ Hartz, VP, Corporate Development at Ansys.*

Early detection is the best way to maximize the value of your business. This will help you make the necessary preparations to make your business more appealing. Early preparations will also help increase the likelihood of a sale. A broken deal can be devastating for a business, as it will have horrible repercussions on employees and even customers.

Benefits of Early Preparation

"The more time you can give yourself to prepare the business for sale, the more successful the sale will be.

If you think about a couple of the things that could be value detractors from a buyer's point of view, let's say you have contracts with unlimited liability, if you're starting long enough in advance, you might be able to modify those contracts over time. So, when there's a renewal, you can modify the language.

In some cases, you might have a new product that has huge potential. Maybe you need to give it a little time to get some traction in the market. You're not just stating that the product is going to be extremely valuable in the future, but there are early earmarks that show that it is getting traction. It's going to have the kind of growth potential that you're putting into your financials or at least into your pitch.

There's a lot of cleanup work that probably goes into this and I start with the theme of knowing myself. I don't want to be in a situation, as a seller of a business, to have the people doing the due diligence on the business know more about it than I do and discover things that I didn't know about, and I'm caught flat-footed. And if I'm surprised, then the buyer starts to be paranoid or questioning everything that's going on with the information we're providing."

— Larry Forman, Senior Manager at Deloitte

Section 6.2 — Preparation

Unless you are doing a fire sale, preparing for a divestiture can take up to six months, or even a year, depending on circumstances. There's a lot of early preparation involved, and each of stage is just as important as the next one. Remember that the more you plan, the higher your chances of deal success.

Deal Perimeter

The first thing to identify is what you are trying to sell. Is it a product? Is it intellectual property? Is it an entire business? Which contract will go with it? Lease agreements, partnership agreements, and many others. Clearly defining this will dictate what the next moves should be. Whatever it is you are trying to sell is part of a larger organization, and you need to set up a deal perimeter and identify which will be part of the sale process and which is not.

Ring Fencing

Another important part of divestiture is identifying who to include in the sale process. This is commonly called ring-fencing. They are a huge value driver of a business, and you may need to put some retention or bonuses in place to keep them on board. At the end of the day, the management team helps sell the business, and without their coopera-tion, it's not going to be a very successful sale, unless the buyer is buying a pure IP asset.

Financials

After identifying the business for sale and the people that come with it, come up with pro forma financial statements and show them the per-formance of the business. The business for sale was a part of a larger entity. therefore, it will not have standalone financials.

Pro Forma Financials on Divestiture

"So, when you're doing a carve-out, those are always complex at some level because most of the time, what you're selling has rarely been presented as a whole, financially, apart from the parents.

Even if you're disposing of an entire segment, it's rare that you're building a complete standalone set of financial statements for that exact business being sold.

So, when you're doing the corporate carve-out, by definition, you are preparing and marketing a business that's never been looked at on a standalone basis. And the management team or the finance team hasn't ever pulled together that complete set of financial historical information aligned to exactly what's being sold."

— Neal McNamara, Co-Founder of Virtas Partners

You can even go as far as conducting research on the potential buyer's capability, creating pro forma financials for their model, and what they could possibly do with your business. Exploring the potential of the business under new ownership is one of the best ways to convince the buyer to acquire your business.

Vendor Due Diligence

This is a growing trend these days as more and more sellers are conducting due diligence on their own companies. It helps reduce surprises that the buyer might see and can increase the likelihood of a sale.

Having everything already prepared when the buyer comes in also reduces their negotiating power and speeds up the entire sale process.

Conducting due diligence on your own company also helps you identify the right time to sell your business, such as bad contracts that have unlimited liabilities, or key milestones in your business that could increase the sale value. All of these things could contribute to the right timing to sell.

Quality of Earnings

Do a quality earnings report to validate the earning stream of a business. Whether you are a buyer or a seller, generating a quality earnings report should be a part of your process, as this will help you understand the real revenue and expenses of the business.

When you build a quality earnings report, you take off one-time events from the financial statements. For instance, a big lawsuit settlement, whether you got paid or you are the one paying, will not be a recurring event. Remove this instantly from the report and any other things that are not part of the normal operation of the business. The entire purpose of the quality of earnings is to create a picture of what the business operation looks like and how much revenue it generates, even if ownership has changes.

Basic Principle of Quality of Earnings

"Quality of earnings is when company A is trying to buy company B and they're trying to validate the earning stream of that particular company. Looking at least two years and a trailing 12-month period, trying to understand the revenue stream and the expense stream.

We take everything down to EBITDA, which is earnings before interest, taxes, and depreciation, and then start to think through different adjustments that are one-time events. That would then give credence to the value that has been placed upon the company that is ultimately going to be purchased.

For the quality of earnings, we're trying to remove one-time, non-recurring, extraordinary items. We are removing those and trying t

---

understand the business. What does the business look like, on a normal run rate without any type of calamity that's happened?

We also take out revenue. One of the largest customers was in the trailing 12-month period and they just lost a customer, who was a 20% customer. The loss of one large customer will affect your operations. In this case, you remove the revenue and the cost of the goods sold that would go with that particular one. Therefore, you're basically effectively removing the margin. You want to make sure you're normalizing and taking out any of these large types of events."

— Andy Jordan, Director at Cohen & Company

It can be extremely beneficial for sellers to prepare their own quality earnings reports. This will help prepare for the buyer's due diligence and can reduce surprises that they may find out. It will also help you have a better expectation of pricing. Knowing the true revenue will help you gauge and negotiate for a better price for your business.

If done correctly and honestly, doing your own quality of earnings can help speed up the process of the sale. The buyer will most likely do their own QofE report, but if they see that you did yours properly, they may opt not to do their own and proceed with the deal.

Importance of Quality of Earnings

"It's in the seller's best interest to do a quality of earnings analysis. The reason is, it prepares them to understand what their true earnings potential is and what their historical run rate has been. It also mitigates another firm coming in and doing a quality of earnings and finding adjustments that they didn't know about.

If the seller comes to the table with their own QofE and their own analysis, it puts the seller at an advantage. Being able to understand

> *what their true quality of earnings is going to allow them to negotiate higher and better returns.*
>
> *You don't want surprises at the end of the day or surprises throughout the process. You want to understand what your quality of earnings is, and what your earnings potential is going into a transaction. And then, if there's discrepancies or thoughts about it, you're well-armed to understand and explain that better to the potential buyer."*
>
> **— Andy Jordan, Director at Cohen & Company**

Alignment

Even with preparations, you can only start a formal sale process and involve the buyer, if everyone is onboard in selling the business. You cannot have conflicting parties internally, especially on the executive level of the organization. If there are people that don't want to sell the business, they can disrupt the entire procedure. If they are a part owner, they might not sign the documents, which will make the sale process futile.

Section 6.3 — Process

Whether you choose to hire a banker or not, the next step after rigorous preparation is to actually find a potential buyer. If you opt to use a banker, they will guide you and help create an auction process. If not, then you need to create your own auction process in order to maximize the value of your business.

Auction

You want to create some competition for your sale. Collect potential buyers and educate them on what you are truly selling. Start by looking within the ecosystem of the business. Partners, customers, or anyone that touches the business can be a potential buyer. From there, you can start moving outwards.

Pull together the virtual data room and start populating it so that the buyers will have a glimpse of what it is they are buying. As they get more serious, start providing more information. During this time, you should also be preparing your confidential information memorandum (CIM).

If a buyer is serious about looking at your business, have them sign an NDA before sharing the CIM. You don't want buyers talking to everyone about confidential information about your company.

At this point, you are now ready to collect offers from serious buyers. Narrow this field to a small handful of parties, and you have reached a different level of negotiations. Confirmatory diligence is next until you reach final negotiations.

Choosing Buyers

Choosing buyers will completely be under the seller's discretion. However, choosing solely based on the price may not be a good idea. There are many factors to consider when choosing the new owner of your business.

Strategic Relationships

One of the things to consider when choosing a buyer is strategic relationships that could benefit your company in the long run. Russ Hartz has a very good example here:

> ## Example of Strategic Relationship Post-Close
>
> *"For example, you're going to sell a software business to a company that has better expertise in that software, they can support it better and they can evolve it better than you can, over time.*
>
> *But they only play in the U.S. They have no salesforce outside of the United States. And you do. You have a global Salesforce.*
>
> *What you might want to do as part of the sale is, you sell the software business to them, they're going to support the customers, et cetera. But as part of the deal, you become their reseller for that software outside of the United States.*
>
> *So that way, you maintain some connection to those customers. You maintain a connection to the buyer for the business, you gain another continuing revenue stream associated with the resale outside the U.S.*
>
> *So, it's much bigger than just the price. There are some strategic considerations, some of which can be made part of the deal."*
>
> **— Russ Hartz, VP, Corporate Development at Ansys.**

Employee Consideration

Remember that choosing the buyer for your business would also mean choosing the next home for the employees. Perhaps, some of the employees have been with your company for a long time. It's only fair that you take care of them, even if you're planning on separating from them.

A happy workforce also translates to increased productivity. If employees are not happy with where they are going, the business that you sold will most likely be in jeopardy. All of these things will contribute to your reputation as you go forward beyond this deal. If you have a reputation of selling failing businesses, or employees don't want to work for your company because of how you treated them, your company will have trouble selling the business the next time around.

> ## Employee Transition on Divestiture
>
> *"We want our employees to have a good transition experience. It's good for everyone. We know that an engaged workforce is a productive workforce. It adds value to the deal. The buyer expects it. We certainly wouldn't want to send them a business that's limping along.*
>
> *We want to put the energy and effort into this that we would expect the buyer to be putting into it. And at the end of the day, it's just the right thing to do."*
>
> **— Sallie Cunningham, Director, People M&A at Apple**

Certainty of Closing

Last, but probably the most important of all, is a certainty to close. It's probably best that you go with the buyer with the highest probability of closing the deal. A huge offer will mean nothing if the sale doesn't come through.

A failed deal can also be devastating to a company. Repercussions can include a strain in relationships between leadership and the employees included in the deal, and also the customers. Imagine how customers might feel if they found out you tried to sell their contract and had to still deal with them because the deal didn't come through.

Section 6.4 — Communication

To avoid strain in relationships altogether, a proper communication plan is key. You don't want to be the villain in the story where you just threw away employees and customers that apparently, you don't want/need anymore. This is not a good look for any company.

Furthermore, employees are a big value driver for the deal. You need their cooperation and eagerness to continue working at the business, even under new management. Have an open and honest conversation with the people. Explain to them why you are selling the business and why it is actually better for them.

Change management is one of the most crucial parts of any deal. If done correctly, you can generate excitement for the employees to go to the new company.

Communicating Divestiture

"There should be a compelling reason for doing the deal. The buyer may be interested in making a particular investment in the business that we haven't. Maybe the business is a better strategic fit with the buyer than it is with us.

Having a credible leadership team in place in this business segment that's being sold, who can articulate good reasons for doing the deal, will help drive the engagement.

And when the employees see the leadership team excited about the future, they will be more inclined to follow. And certainly, wherever the buyer is willing and able to be part of the announcement or other milestones that occur pre-close, employees will be listening intently for both what is said and not said.

It's also important to just put employees' minds at ease with things like having a communication strategy. That includes what the basic outbound terms and conditions will be for the treatment of their benefits.

Honestly, you can generate excitement about the future of the business. But only once the employee's basic needs are met. If we think about it as if we're part of a transaction ourselves as an employee, once you know you're going to have a job, be able to cover your household expenses,

---

and provide insurance for yourself and your family. Once you have those basic needs met, then you can focus on the future of the business.

So, this is all part of that overall strategy that the buyer needs to be thinking of very early on so that they can help provide those types of reassurances."

— Sallie Cunningham, Director, People M&A at Apple

Communication with customers is also important, especially if you will still be dealing with them on other products or services. Reassure them that they will be in good, if not better, hands, after the sale. And this should also hold true, which is why you should choose the right buyer carefully, as mentioned before.

Section 6.5 — TSA

Because the asset is not a standalone business and is usually a part of a larger organization, the buyer might not be able to operate the business immediately post-close. This is where transitional service agreements (TSA) come in.

In a nutshell, a TSA is there to make sure that the business will run business-as-usual on day one under the new owner. You will be providing the buyer services that they don't currently have, such as payroll services, benefits platforms, or even infrastructures, that are essential to operate their newly acquired business.

The key to a successful TSA is specificity. Figure out what are the things that will be necessary to run the business that the buyer cannot provide immediately, how much to charge for those services, and for how long. Everything needs to be stated clearly in the agreement. TSAs are usually not more than 12 months and are only done as a temporary bridge, while the buyers establish their new business.

Time Limit on TSAs

"And then the key point here, and this is where I've seen a lot of parties on both sides get tripped up, is around the employment of these transition services.

TSAs can't go on forever. You need to set an endpoint. You need to set milestones for how you're going to get to that employment and fully transition the business to the buyer. You should establish regular management, recording, and meetings to check in on the milestones to enforce some discipline. Maybe on a bi-weekly or monthly basis.

So, people, don't just hum along and not think about when do we finish this? And you just need a lot of discipline around your intent and in your actions towards moving the buyer off these services.

And there's conflict internally because you don't want to do anything, as the seller, to disrupt this business even after the buyers take it over. Remember many times, the customers you've transitioned to this buyer, they're going to be your customers too, in other contexts. Or you may have transitioned some partners that are also your partners in other contexts.

So, you don't want to do anything that damages the business that you've sold. Cause it may end up impacting some of your own continuing customers and partners. So, there is this internal conflict you want to support. You want to be helpful. You want to see that the business stood up on its own with the new buyer. But you're not running a charity and you need to do something with your own resources in the long-term as well."

— Russ Hartz, VP, Corporate Development at Ansys.

Here is a play on how to negotiate and finalize a TSA before signing and closing:

Play # 13 — Final TSA & Costing

❖ **Description:** Use this play to learn how to negotiate and finalize a divestiture's TSA before signing and closing.

❖ **Play by:** Toby Tester

About the play

It's not uncommon to find that the TSA is the last transaction document to be finalized before signing and closing. The document should be negotiated, taking into account both the buyer's and seller's interests. The TSA will have a complete list of all transition-related services provided that covers the following:

- **What services are Delivered:** This articulates the set of services the receiver will obtain from the service provider.

- **Who is the Service Provider and Receiver:** This identifies the legal entities that will provide and receive services.

- **How Long Is the Service Going to Be Provided For:** The duration of each service element, along with allowed extensions, should be made transparent to both the service provider and receiver.

- **Service Provider and Receiver Obligations:** Delineates key aspects of the service that are dependent on key activities performed by the service provider or receiver to trigger, set up, and deliver the service.

Preparation

People: Executive sponsor, separation manager, and deal team

Difficulty: Medium

Materials: Meeting Agenda, Whiteboard, Strategy Documents

Time: Spend one day or more preparing materials for a two-hour play.

Running the Play:

1. Confirm Service Levels

   The TSA should describe service performance levels for each of the service elements, as well as specifications for all measures to be adopted for service-level monitoring and the agreed-upon frequency for measurement and reporting activities.

   The Service Level should cover:

   - Services subject to the SLA
   - Metrics (e.g., 99% availability of mission-critical systems)
   - Measurement approach

2. Finalize Service Costs and Payment Terms

   A clear definition of all service costs, costing methodologies, and invoicing procedures should be documented in the TSA as follows:

   Break down service costs by service elements.

   - Methodology on how the costs are determined

- Use unit charges, rate cards, and volume metrics for cost methodology

- Adjustments (i.e., true-up or true-down) in costs that align with changes in scope

- Payment terms, such as frequency of invoicing, incremental costs

- Agreed Ownership, Communication, and Reporting

Each TSA in-scope service is operationally managed and delivered by a TSA owner from the service provider. The TSA owner is also responsible for providing regular reports on service performance to the receiver. A list of such reports, including audit reports, reporting frequency, and a recipient list, should be clearly articulated in the TSA document. An outline of the procedures to report and escalate problems must also be defined and documented to support the overall governance model during TSA execution.

3. Define the TSA Governance

The divestiture governance process needs to take into account how to govern TSA post-close. The most critical roles required as part of the governance model include:

Executive Management

- This is the highest level of decision-making authority within the governance model. Executive management handles issue escalation, mitigation, and dispute management.

TSA Owners

- They define and refine TSA management processes, identify and mitigate TSA delivery risks, and help manage financial commitments and exits. The managers also work closely with TSA owners to report execution status and to escalate issues through the right channels.

TSA Billing

This group is responsible for compiling monthly status updates from TSA owners, coordinating with billing teams for invoicing and collections, and tracking and reporting progress toward TSA exits.

Need-Based Support

These are specialized teams that support TSA execution on an as-needed basis and include representatives from:

- **Legal:** Legal support for interpretation and issue resolution

- **Finance:** Support for payments and collections

- **Tax:** Advisory support on tax implications

4. Finalize Billing Management

Set up billing for TSA services in advance. The process involves identifying the cost centers to bill for each service at an appropriate level of aggregation (i.e., local, regional, global). Define a billing threshold criterion appropriate for the billing frequency (e.g., quarterly billing for more than $5000) in the TSA invoicing. Timeframes required for filing and resolving billing disputes should also be defined in the TSA invoicing and payment terms.

Conclusion

Standing up an M&A function has many twists and turns. This book is written from the perspective of two key personas: a CEO and a new head of corporate development. These main actors come to life in the decisions, thoughts, and considerations of each chapter. As the CEO, you have an exciting future with corporate development in your leadership ranks. However, don't forget to provide continuous support, since this new team does not run autonomously. As the head of corporate development, you have to maintain a healthy balance between strategist and operator in the beginning.

I wrote this book with the heartfelt intention of sharing my knowledge and contributions from the community. It is 'our' knowledge: a collection of practical advice from us in the industry. We want you to take what we've learned and turn it into early successes. Whether you are the CEO-reader or the corp dev-reader, there are plenty of examples we placed in this book, so you would not have to rebuild what is already out there.

During the writing of this book, I still received requests from customers for guidance in building out their M&A function. I did my best to quickly add any new content before my publisher closed me out. {grin} Mark Twain said it best "Continuous improvement is better than delayed perfection." There are still plenty of tactical lessons and chapters to add to this book. I cannot claim that this book is the only reference you should have on your shelf. As a matter of fact, if your company is investing in the creation of an M&A team, then you will want to look at several books out there, talk to as many practitioners as possible, review as many software tools you have time for, and checkout podcasts during your downtime.

"Continuous improvement is better than delayed perfection." – Mark Twain

---

My co-author and I firmly believe that the heart of this community is in sharing. This book is practical guidance and learnings from those who've been around a while. We offer this to you as a new joiner to our community. Welcome to the M&A community.

Cheers to you and your first deal.

About the Authors

Kison Patel is the Founder and CEO of M&A Science, paving the future of M&A with educational resources, an inclusive community environment, and technology platforms. He hosts the industry's leading M&A podcast and founded the M&A Science Academy, a self-paced training program featuring lessons and techniques from top practitioners. Kison also founded DealRoom, an M&A lifecycle management platform. He is also the author of Agile M&A: Proven Techniques to Close Deals Faster and Maximize Value.

John Morada is a 17-year veteran in corporate development and the Chief Operating Officer at M&A Science. Prior to joining M&A Science and DealRoom, John served as an integration leader in multiple companies, public and private. He understands the evolution of integration methodologies is a natural progression through philosophy, communication, and understanding. That is why he is the champion for Agile M&A Integration as a modern framework for current and future generations of Integration practitioners.

Appendix

1. Evolving Your Corporate Development Function
   Michael Palumbo, Director of Corporate Development, HALO
   Branded Solutions https://www.mascience.com/library/evolving-your-corporate-development-function

2. Working with the Business Leader to Build an M&A Strategy
   Michael Frankel, SVP and Managing Director, Deloitte New-venture Accelerator / Deloitte Investments
   https://www.mascience.com/library/working-with-the-business-leader-to-build-an-m-a-strategy

3. Hunting deals in M&A Dustin Intihar, Director, M&A and
   Strategic Partnerships at Enprotech Corp
   https://www.mascience.com/library/hunting-deals-in-m-a

4. Behind the Scenes: Effective Deal Sourcing and Closing
   Scott Kaeser, Head of Corporate Development at First Choice
   Dental Lab https://www.mascience.com/library/behind-the-scenes-effective-deal-sourcing-and-closing

5. Aligning Strategy with Your M&A Process
   Sean Corcoran, Senior VP, Corporate Development & M&A at
   DigiCert, Inc. https://www.mascience.com/library/aligning-strategy-with-your-m-a-process

6. How to Successfully Build a Corporate Development Function
   Nichelle Maynard-Elliott, Independent Board Director at Xerox
   www.mascience.com/library/how-to-successfully-build-a-corporate-development-function

7. Building a Corporate Development Function From Scratch
    Russ Hartz, VP, Corporate Development at Ansys
    www.mascience.com/library/building-a-corporate-development-function-from-scratch

8. Turning a Deal Thesis into Integration Objectives
    Christian Von Bogdandy, Senior Director at Slalom
    https://www.mascience.com/courses/turning-a-deal-thesis-into-integration-objectives

9. Why is M&A Integration so Hard?
    James Timothy Payne, Principal Consultant at Merger Integration Consulting, LLC
    www.mascience.com/library/why-is-m-a-integration-so-hard

10. Why is M&A Integration so Hard?
    Galina Wolinetz, Managing Director at Virtas Partners M&A Integration | Separations
    www.mascience.com/library/why-is-m-a-integration-so-hard

11. Common Divestiture Challenges and How to Overcome Them
    Kelly Haggerty, Founder of Nearco Transaction Advisors, LLC.
    https://www.mascience.com/library/common-divestiture-challenges-and-how-to-overcome-them

12. How to Implement an Agile Approach into M&A
    James Harris, Principal, Corporate Development Integration at Google
    www.mascience.com/library/how-to-implement-an-agile-approach-into-m-a

13. How Proactive Integration Engagement Can Differentiate Value in Deals
    Johanna Tseng, Corporate Development, M&A Integration at

Coinbase
www.mascience.com/library/how-proactive-integration-
engagement-can-differentiate-value-in-deals

14. How to Drive Transformational Change Through M&A
Toby Tester, Senior Consultant and Project Manager at BTD
www.mascience.com/library/how-to-drive-transformational-
change-through-m-a

15. The Role and Impact of Leadership in M&A
Dr. J. Keith Dunbar, CEO/Founder of JKD Talent Solutions
and FedLearn
www.mascience.com/library/the-role-and-impact-of-leadership-
in-m-a

16. How to Commit to Integration from Start to Finish
Karen Ashley, Vice President, Corporate Development
Integration at Cisco
https://www.mascience.com/library/how-to-commit-to-
integration-from-start-to-finish

17. Deal Origination from a PE Investor's Perspective
Jay Jester, Partner at Plexus Capital, LLC
https://www.mascience.com/library/deal-origination-from-a-pe-
investors-perspective

18. Transforming M&A to Improve Integration
Javid Moosaji, M&A Sales Integration Strategy at Paypal
https://www.mascience.com/library/transforming-m-a-to-
improve-integration

19. The Legal Team's Role in M&A
Andrew Gratz, Associate General Counsel at LyondellBasell
https://www.mascience.com/library/the-legal-teams-role-in-m-a

20. The HR Practitioner's Guide to M&A Due Diligence
    Klint Kendrick, HR M&A Leader with several Fortune 500 firms
    http://www.mascience.com/library/the-hr-practitioners-guide-to-mergers-acquisitions-due-diligence

21. Building a Corporate Development Team with Contingencies
    Jeremy Segal, Senior Vice President of Corporate Development at Progress
    www.mascience.com/library/how-to-build-and-align-a-corporate-development-team-with-multiple-mandates

22. How Successful Diligence and Integration Planning Frames Successful M&A and Valuation
    Erik Levy, Group Head Corp Dev, and M&A at DMGT PLC
    www.mascience.com/library/how-successful-diligence-and-integration-planning-frames-successful-m-a-and-valuation

23. Aligning People in M&A for a Better Outcome
    Carlos Cesta, Vice President, Corporate Development/M&A at Presidio
    www.mascience.com/library/aligning-people-in-m-a-for-a-better-outcome

24. Managing a Multi-Vertical M&A Strategy
    Jerry Will, VP of Corporate Development at 3M
    www.mascience.com/library/managing-a-multi-vertical-m-a-strategy

25. Transformative M&A
    Duncan Painter, CEO of Ascential
    https://www.mascience.com/library/transformative-m-a

26. Bridging the Gap Between Corporate Development and Integration
Devorah Bertucci, Director, Corporate Development at Microsoft
www.mascience.com/library/bridging-the-gap-between-corporate-development-and-integration

27. From Private to Public Company
Darren Lampert, CEO at GrowGeneration Corp
https://www.mascience.com/library/how-to-prevent-international-from-failing

28. How to Build an M&A Communication Plan
David Olsson, Partner at Beyond the Deal
https://www.mascience.com/courses/constructing-an-m-a-communication-plan

29. Building an Effective Internal Communication Plan for M&A
Briana Elkington, Sr. Manager, M&A Integration Management Office at Community Psychiatry
www.mascience.com/library/building-an-effective-internal-communication-plan-for-m-a

30. Preserving Value in M&A
Jay Dettling, CEO of Ansira
https://www.mascience.com/library/how-to-preserve-value-in-m-a

31. Assessing Value Realization
Mike Devita, Success Strategy Lead at Salesforce
https://www.mascience.com/library/assessing-value-realization

32. Structuring Talent-Focused Acquisitions
Christina Ungaro, Head of Corporate Development at JLL
www.mascience.com/library/structuring-talent-focused-
acquisitions

33. How to Successfully Execute Deals with a Small Team
Jason Lippert, CEO of LCI Industries
https://www.mascience.com/library/how-to-successfully-execute-
deals-with-a-small-team

34. Managing M&A on a High Scale
Jeff Bender, CEO at Harris
https://www.mascience.com/library/managing-m-a-on-a-high-
scale

35. How to Build an M&A Center of Excellence from Scratch
Philip Pratt, Director, Acquisition Integration at Corning
Incorporated
www.mascience.com/library/how-to-build-an-m-a-center-of-
excellence-from-scratch

36. Divestitures: Planning to Execution
Larry Forman, Senior Manager at Deloitte
https://www.mascience.com/courses/planning-and-executing-a-
divestiture

37. How To Plan a Divestiture From an Accounting Perspective
Neal McNamara, Co-Founder of Virtas Partners
www.mascience.com/library/how-to-plan-a-divestiture-from-an-
accounting-perspective

38. The Importance of Conducting a Quality of Earnings in M&A
    Andy Jordan, Director at Cohen & Company
    www.mascience.com/library/the-importance-of-conducting-a-
    quality-of-earnings-in-m-a

39. How to Build a Divestiture from HR's Perspective
    Sallie Cunningham, Director, People M&A at Apple
    www.mascience.com/library/how-to-build-a-divestiture-from-hrs-
    perspective

40. Why Big Companies Destroy Small Ones
    Jeff Desroches, Vice President, Strategy & Corporate Develop-
    ment at VAT GROUP
    http://www.mascience.com/library/why-big-companies-destroy-
    small-ones

41. Navigating International Deals
    Jeff Baker, Chief Financial Officer at Paysign, Inc.
    https://www.mascience.com/library/navigating-international-
    deals

42. The Importance of Conducting Cultural Assessments
    Dawn White, Program Manager at Corning Incorporated
    www.mascience.com/library/mergers-and-acquisitions-cultural-
    assessments

43. Assimilating Unique Cultures in M&A
    Kim Jones, Sr. HR M&A Manager at Microsoft
    https://www.mascience.com/library/assimilating-unique-cultures-
    in-m-a

44. How to succeed in M&A integration and measure that success
   Jim Buckley, Vice President, Mergers and Acquisitions
   Integration at VMware
   https://www.mascience.com/library/how-to-succeed-in-m-a-
   integration-and-measure-success

45. Managing M&A Sourcing, Diligence and Integration
   Sabeeh Khan, Director, Corporate Strategy & Development at
   Syniti
   https://www.mascience.com/library/managing-m-a-sourcing-
   diligence-and-integration

46. Managing M&A Sourcing, Diligence and Integration
   Aaron Whiting, M&A Integration and Strategic Programs at
   ContinuumCloud
   https://www.mascience.com/library/managing-m-a-sourcing-
   diligence-and-integration

47. How to Negotiate and Structure NDAs
   Mark Khavkin, CFO at Pantheon Platform
   https://www.mascience.com/library/the-secret-to-a-successful-nda

48. Buy or Build Considerations in M&A
   Cameron Weiner, VP of Strategic Development, Head of M&A
   at Shopko Optical
   https://www.mascience.com/library/buy-or-build-considerations

49. Hiring your Head of Corp Dev that Fits your Strategy
   Charles Breed, VP of Corporate Development at Corel
   Corporation
   https://www.mascience.com/library/hiring-the-head-of-corp-dev-
   that-fits-your-m-a-strategy

50. How to Structure Teams Approaching Diligence
Ken Bond, Head of Corporate Development at Cetera Financial
Group
https://www.mascience.com/library/how-to-structure-teams-
approaching-diligence

51. Making M&A GTM Successful
Gwen Pope, Head of Global Product M&A at eBay
https://www.mascience.com/library/making-m-a-gtm-successful

52. How To Approach Diligence
Ben Sutton, Director, Corporate Development at Equifax
https://www.mascience.com/courses/m-a-science-diligence-
management-certification

53. Hiring your Head of Corporate Development Team
Justin Goldman, CFO at Place Exchange
https://www.mascience.com/courses/hiring-your-corporate-
development-team

54. Creating the right governance structure in M&A deals
Tomer Stavitsky, Corporate Development, M&A Lead at
Intuitive Surgical
https://www.mascience.com/library/creating-the-right-
governance-structure-in-an-m-a-deal

55. How to Modernize a Process-Based Company
Naomi O'Brien, Head of M&A Integration at Honeywell
https://www.mascience.com/podcast/how-to-modernize-a-
process-based-company

56. Evolving Your M&A Integration Function
Christina Amiry, Chief of Staff to the COO at Atlassian
https://www.mascience.com/library/evolving-your-m-a-
integration-function

57. Standing up a Diligence and Integration Management Office
Kerry Perez, Head of Diligence and Integration Management
Office (M&A) at AMN Healthcare
https://www.mascience.com/podcast/standing-up-a-diligence-
and-integration-management-office

58. How To Pivot to an M&A Integration Career
John Morada, COO at M&A Science
https://www.mascience.com/podcast/how-to-pivot-to-an-m-a-
integration-career

59. Sourcing Companies That Are Not for Sale
Rishabh Mishra, Vice President and Head of Corporate
Development at Infostretch
https://www.mascience.com/podcast/sourcing-companies-that-
are-not-for-sale

Made in the USA
Las Vegas, NV
29 August 2024

94601781R00118